SEEING WITH MY EYES CLOSED

SEEING WITH MY EYES CLOSED

INSIGHTS FROM MOMENTS OF MEDITATION

MANISH CHOPRA, PhD

EMBASSY BOOKS
www.embassybooks.in

First Indian Edition, Published in 2024 by:
Embassy Book Distributors
120, Great Western Building, Maharashtra Chamber of Commerce Lane, Fort, Mumbai 400 023, India
Tel: (+9122) -30967415, 22819546
Email: info@embassybooks.in
www.embassybooks.in

ISBN: 978-81-19729-82-1

Distribution Centres:
Mumbai, Ahmedabad, Bangalore, Kolkata, Chennai, Hyderabad, New Delhi, Pune

Printed & bound in India by Repro India Ltd.,
Navi Mumbai

Dedication

This book is dedicated to my daughter, Leela.
Her emergence into our lives has been
a source of boundless joy.

Contents

Uncommon Commonsense

Inscrutable Mind

Introduction

The concept of this book came about several years ago when I observed insights emerging spontaneously during periods of silent meditation. Introspective contemplation producing wisdom wasn't a surprise, yet the unexpected and effortless nature of certain deeper mysteries of life revealing themselves was startling and have left a lasting imprint on my mind.

Many of the ideas expressed in the pages that follow may not all be new to the reader nor inherently original to me. I chose to share them because even timeless truths have come up in new and powerful ways for me since I devoted myself to a life of meditation. And importantly, they have all emerged in the form of practical wisdom in correlation with lived experiences that have made them memorable and meaningful.

There are three principal ways in which we imbibe new learning. The first is wisdom acquired from someone else's experiences. The second is intellectualized knowledge that arises from one's own logical analysis and inferences drawn from external information. The third is through firsthand experience. Naturally, this last one leaves the most indelible impression on the mind and has the potential to transform one's mindset and behavior because it is truly and most deeply internalized.

The purpose of sharing these insights is two-fold: to pass on beneficial ideas and life-lessons that have arisen in moments of meditation, and importantly, to encourage the reader to introduce (or enhance, as the case might be) a practice of contemplation in their lives, which would bestow similar bounties upon them directly.

One might ask why a contemplative practice like meditation yields such spontaneous, valuable, and lasting insights.

The simplest analogy I offer is that of a kettle filled with water that is placed on a source of energy like a gas burner or electric stove. Once you turn on the ignition, it is only a matter of time until the water will start to heat up and generate steam. The steam is akin to the emergent insights and the energy source is the regular practice of contemplation or meditation.

What is fascinating is that once the source of energy is activated, one doesn't need to put in any extra special effort to make sure that the liquid water will turn into vapor. It is the law of nature (thermodynamics) that will turn matter from one form to another through transfer of energy. The introduction of Vipassana meditation is the metaphorical "energy source" in my own context.

I am grateful that these insights have emerged in my mind and provided me much needed guidance and self-direction at critical life junctures and on a day-to-day basis. I hope others might draw benefit from the ideas expressed in this book and be inspired to pursue their own paths to enrich their lives with self-discovery.

Vipassana Meditation

Vipassana, which means to see things as they really are, is one of India's most ancient techniques of meditation. It was rediscovered by Gautama Buddha more than 2,500 years ago and was taught by him as a universal remedy for universal ills.

This non-sectarian technique aims for the total eradication of mental impurities and the resultant highest happiness and complete liberation. Its purpose is healing—not merely the curing of diseases but the essential healing of human suffering.

Vipassana is a simple and powerful way of self-transformation through self-observation. It focuses on the deep interconnection between mind and body, which can be experienced directly by disciplined attention to the physical sensations that form the life of the body, and that continuously interconnect and condition the life and nature of the mind.

It is an observation-based, self-explanatory journey into the interplay between mind and body. Its regular and dedicated practice removes mental defilements, resulting in a balanced mind full of equanimity, love, and compassion.

The scientific laws that operate one's thoughts, feelings, judgements, and intentions become clear and self-evident. Through direct experience, the nature of how one grows or regresses, how one produces suffering or frees oneself from suffering is understood. A deep self-realization emerges that we are responsible for our own happiness through the actions of our mind, body, and speech. Life becomes characterized by increased awareness, non-delusion, self-control, and peace.

Since the time of the Buddha to present day, Vipassana has been handed down in its pure form through an unbroken chain of teachers. The technique was largely maintained and taught by ordained monks and their monastic disciples, but has always been readily available for householders to learn and practice as well.

Only in the last two centuries, the privilege to disseminate Vipassana was granted to hand-picked householders by some of the more progressive monks who embraced the idea of the liberating technique reaching and appealing to a wider populace. One such teacher was Sayagyi U Ba Khin (1899-1971), who was a high-ranking Burmese government official and had been taught by a farmer, Saya Thetgyi (1873-1949), who was appointed by the Venerable Ledi Sayadaw (1846-1923) to allow greater access to householders.

The most recent principal teacher in this lineage is the late S.N. Goenka (1924-2013). Ethnically Indian yet born and raised in Burma (present-day Myanmar), he had the good fortune to learn Vipassana from Sayagyi U Ba Khin. After 14 years of Sayagyi's disciplined tutelage in Burma, after his first course in 1955, Mr. Goenka (fondly and respectfully known as Goenkaji) settled in India and began teaching Vipassana in 1969.

His initial intent was to simply teach Vipassana to his parents and some close family members upon arriving in India. Once initiated, however, the demand for him to continue teaching the powerful technique kept growing in a spontaneous and exponential manner.

He went on to directly teach tens of thousands of people of all races and religions in both the East and the West until his passing in 2013. In 1982, he began appointing assisting teachers (AT) to help meet the growing demand for Vipassana courses, which are currently taught in the format of residential retreats in over 200 dedicated locations around the world.

More information about Vipassana meditation as taught by S.N. Goenka, including centers where it is taught free of charge in its pristine form, can be found on www.dhamma.org.

Personal Practice and Emergence

I consider myself very fortunate to have encountered Vipassana meditation in my life and its regular practice continues to benefit me immensely. Each individual's path in life (mundane or spiritual) is unique and incomparable. I share some background on my contemplative practice to provide the reader some context for the source of ideas expressed in this book.

I attended my first Vipassana retreat at the end of 2010 and have since been practicing it regularly. That translates into meditating daily for at least an hour (typically in the morning) and often for an additional 30 to 60 minutes in the evening. This is complemented annually by a residential retreat like the very first one that introduced me to the technique. There are days and years when it feels much harder to maintain my commitment to the practice, much as the case might be for sticking to a healthy lifestyle with physical fitness.

Slowly and gradually, with intention and purpose, I regain the strength and confidence to continue on this beneficial and joyous path. And while it often feels like starting something all over again as a complete novice, the efficacy of the technique quickly shines through and re-grounds me to maintain my discipline to continue pursuing it.

In the interest of space and to avoid repetition, I refer the reader to my first book, *The Equanimous Mind,* which chronicles my initial experience and ongoing practice of Vipassana meditation.

Emergence by its very nature is spontaneous and thus hard to pin down into a specific mold or exact procedural sequence. That powerful and self-generated insights will emerge through contemplation is but guaranteed because it is the stillness and the silence that allows these perspectives to surface up through the sludge of commonplace existence. And yet one can't program this into a precisely repeatable occurrence every time one takes a seat on the cushion to meditate.

Flowers will bloom in time—sometimes in overnight spurts, sometimes in days long micro-movements—and yet, springtime and fertile conditions all but guarantee their emergence, timed to perfection.

If you are exploring adding a contemplative practice to your life and find an added incentive through the prospect of arriving at self-discovered personal insights, I encourage you to be patient and playful with the possibilities.

A Note to the Reader

This book is written in the form of short distinct vignettes that each present an insightful gem. I have organized them into loosely defined sections, but you may choose to explore them in any order and in a piecemeal manner.

Each vignette stands alone but there are often common threads that run through several of them. Wherever possible and logical, I have noted which others correlate with the one being perused, should you want to enjoy them together.

The gems classified under *Abstractions Expounded* are relatively well-known concepts to the spiritually inclined and those attuned with their inner worlds. The purpose of clarifying the embodiment of these concepts is to serve them up with universal appeal and offer elaborations based on personal experience.

Uncommon Commonsense vignettes are, as the section header conveys, ideas that may be well known yet perhaps less well understood or internalized. Some other vignettes represent an ideology from the mundane world that has an application in the spiritual realm as well. Yet others are newer ideas that need fresh acknowledgement, definition, and elaboration.

The *Inscrutable Mind* section aims to demystify paradoxical concepts and explore other provocative insights that offer perspective on the conundrums one faces in life in general, and in the pursuit of inner wisdom. *This Lifetime* vignettes serve to inspire, if not spur, the reader into a healthy sense of seriousness and urgency on pursuing a virtuous path with intention, without delay or further hesitation.

Given the intentionally condensed nature of the writing, it may be easy to skim through the entire matter in one or two sittings. I would encourage ingesting one vignette at a time to allow for greater internalization of the ideas and self-reflection to assess their relevancy and significance for you.

In fact, I invite the conscious reader to treat each vignette as an opportunity for contemplation and introspection. Contribute your own correlated observations, insights, or lived experiences in the *Personal Reflections* spaces provided throughout the book.

I can't promise if the ideas presented in this book seem of immense or immediate value on the surface. I sincerely hope that you allow the possibility to chisel and polish them through your own reflections, and emerge thus with your own insightful gems.

Definitions and Concepts

Emergent

- Arising unexpectedly
- Calling for prompt action
- Arising as a natural or logical consequence
- Newly formed or prominent

Gem

- Jewel
- A precious or sometimes semi-precious stone cut and polished for ornament
- Something prized especially for great beauty or perfection
- A highly prized or well-beloved person

Dhamma

- Fundamental inviolable laws governing universal phenomena
- Reference to the body of Buddha's teachings
- Inherent nature or essential quality of something or someone
- Upholding the universal moral code
- Mental states or phenomena

Karma

- Action in the past and present
- Sum total of one's actions from current and previous states of existence
- Principle that dictates causes have correlated and proportional effects
- Belief that past and present actions determine one's future—in this or subsequent lifetimes

Equanimity

- Mental calmness and equilibrium, especially in a difficult situation
- Stability of mind to withstand ups and downs with composure and evenness of temper

Inner Development

- A sustaining process of tuning one's focus and attention inward through contemplation
- Outcome from regular practice of meditation, introspection, or other spiritual pursuits

The Path

- A reference to the inner journey one must undertake to pursue spiritual awakening
- Specific reference to followership of Buddha's teachings to seek liberation from suffering

Mundane and Supra-mundane

- Mundane refers to worldly matters or materialistic pursuits
- Supra-mundane thus refers to activities or pursuits that transcend the mundane, are spiritual in nature, or beyond the realm of the material world

Cravings and Aversions

- Key tenet of Buddha's teachings that the source of all suffering is either attachment to *ragas* (cravings) or avoidance of *dosas* (aversions)
- Essence of Vipassana meditation to free oneself from cravings and aversions by remaining equanimous when these conditions manifest in the mind and co-arise with bodily sensations, which are either pleasant or unpleasant in nature

Sensations and Mentations

- Sensations are bodily phenomena (e.g., itch, tingle) that accompany any mental conception or the mind's response to external stimuli through the sense doors
- Mentations refer to mental phenomena or the formation of thoughts based on internal or external factors

Defilements and Conditioning

- Defilements are mental impurities (e.g., anger, greed), often the consequence of ego, cravings, or aversions
- Accumulation of defilements creates the conditioning that guide our every action
- De-conditioning the mind to free it from defilements is the only way to seek and achieve peace, equanimity, and liberation from endless suffering

Spirituality and Religion

- Often synonymously used (an easily confused) words but being spiritual (deeply attuned with one's inner self) does not necessarily imply doing so in the context of any organized religion
- The secular meaning of the word "religion" is simply to reflect qualities that imply devotion, discipline, and an empowering /guiding belief system
- Commonplace usage of the word now refers to one of the major organized religions instead of simple adherence to a well-trodden belief system or a powerfully beneficial life pursuit
- Spirituality is not necessarily embedded in following some form of organized religion
- However, most religions ascribe importance to spiritual awakening and outline their own prescribed (and often singular) approach to pursuing it

ABSTRACTIONS EXPOUNDED

When the Student Is Ready, Then the Teacher Appears

The journey towards the final goal simply cannot begin until the "student is ready". My own story is a case in point.

Despite sufficient encouragement, prompting, goading and then insistence from my wife, it took me five long years to give meditation a fair, if a skeptical and reluctant, trial. I was so set in my ways and beliefs that an opportunity staring me in my face was blocked from view due to the veil of ignorance.

And yet, I now believe that one comes into contact with this secret ingredient only when fully ripened, as that is when the learning will imbue and have maximal value. In practical terms, what I mean is that I had to burn further in my own self-created agony in the crucible of life to arrive at the doorstep of the noble learning that leads to living in alignment with the universal principles of existence. In some ways, this is apt and perhaps even a necessary precondition for one to draw maximal benefit and overcome doubt.

I now believe that my own system had to brim up to capacity with the toxicity of how I was living my life on the inside, even as I was outwardly and materially quite successful, for me to be ready and open to a new approach. It was only when I found myself sufficiently answer-less on how to step out of the vicious cycles of cravings and aversions did I even consider a seemingly unscientific approach.

This was not too dissimilar from how I had eventually stumbled upon another seemingly unscientific medical treatment in the form of chiropractic care on prior occasions. This alternative treatment approach had helped to finally alleviate and manage years of chronic back pain which had remained unresolved despite every attempt to treat it with modern approaches to medicine. Much in the same way, I was later able to dissect, understand, and accept the holistic appeal of chiropractic medicine at the level of my scientific understanding, so have I found Vipassana meditation practice to be the most sound, logical, and effective approach to living an equanimous and happy life.

Years hence, I smile when I come across scores of other seekers and travelers on the same or similar path narrating their stories of spontaneous and seemingly coincidental occurrences that led them to unlock the door to inner purification after years of heedlessness and pursuit of mindless escapes.

My explanation for these phenomena is three-fold. First, the futile pursuits that lead to the doorstep of self-discovery are actually part of a helpful process that creates the realization that outward attainments alone don't lead to inner satisfaction and also helps to lower the sense of ego, without which any spiritual pursuit is likely to be unsuccessful. And second, at a more karmic level (which is hard to explain with linear logic), there has to be a certain passage of time for the ripening of the inner seed or more simply put, for shedding the karma that is blocking us from the path of purification. And thus, it is so that only "when the student is ready" in this manner does the teacher (or the pathway) spontaneously appear to impart the learning and make us self-reliant and established on this noble pursuit.

Finally, at a cosmic level, even with all these preconditions being in place, the universe must truly align and welcome the seeker on their path as any effort, howsoever motivated and strong, has to be in coherence with the energy system of nature. Even as the proverbial horse gets repeatedly drawn to the water, does it eventually gulp down bucketfuls to quench its thirst only when its merits are ripened in pursuit.

Scaling the Mountain of Inner Purification, p.147

Personal Reflections

No Coincidences (Or Karmic Connections)

Growing up in the land of superstitions and astrological readings, I have inherited my share of beliefs ranging from a black cat bringing ill-fortune to trying to change destiny through use of certain gem stones which hold the power to alter future life events. I even had my own pseudo-scientific theory to explain away why I would follow the practice of wearing multiple-colored gem stones on specific fingers and set in rings made of suitably correlated metals to derive outcomes like vanquishing adversaries to more mundane ones like preserving good health and amassing a fortune. As I tasted the nectar of objectively observing my mind and body through meditation, I quickly concluded that my destiny wasn't beholden to astrological charts or apparent omens.

In fact, how I choose to thoughtfully respond, blindly react, or remain neutrally observant to the thoughts and their companion physical manifestation, will initiate a positive, negative, or neutral chain reaction of subsequent events. What I now believe, however not as a superstition, is that everything happens for a reason and that there are no random coincidences in this world or universe. And what are the possible reasons for these occurrences?

In short, it is our karma (or accumulation of prior and ongoing actions) that fuels the processes, connections, and outcomes in our life. We may not be able to comprehend or fathom the rationale in the moment given the limitations of our mind to process the multitude of dominos that may have fallen to cause the butterfly effect in that moment for a situation to manifest in a certain inexplicable way. So, when things start to happen that we can't explain—whether sublime or dark in their appeal—they are actually happening in a perfectly orderly manner from the standpoint of the laws of the universe that govern cause and effect.

For instance, people come into our lives at the perfect (or seemingly inopportune) moment, whether to give us joy or to challenge us and help us learn something or give us an opportunity to serve them and earn karmic merit. I no longer feel surprised or remark as coincidental when something that's been weighing on my mind for a long time resolves itself spontaneously. Any sooner or any later wouldn't have been any better and a mathematician couldn't have come up with a more precisely timed solution!

Another simple illustration is the popular "you reap what you sow" ideology which reminds us that the actions (or seeds) from our present (or past) is what will bring the results (or fruits) in the future. Once a certain action has been taken, the resultant outcome is directly governed by its inherent volitional merit and simply cannot be avoided.

I have stopped over-analyzing the "why" and the "when" aspect of these karmic connections as I now understand that the rationale behind them is too profound and has manifested from too many possibilities into alignment.

It has become clear through closer inferential examination over a long time frame that there are higher order processes that guide the aspects of our life that we don't control directly. These higher order processes don't randomly occur. They are guided by the quantum of our previous and current actions. And while I can't go back in time to reverse misdeeds from the past, my current actions constitute the input that I am contributing into the universe and are karmic seeds that I am sowing—good, bad, or neutral—and are generators of the future that I may thus enjoy or suffer

Everything Is Perfectly Timed…, p.19
People Come into Our Lives for a Reason…, p.39

Personal Reflections

Do Nothing and Achieve Everything...
...Do Less and Receive More

Probably the most profound insight and corresponding development I have experienced through deepening my meditation practice is the surprising revelation that the less I do, the more I receive. This is one of the hardest epiphanies to believe without experiencing it firsthand in your life. How does this gem manifest in practical terms?

The essence of this emergence is that when I truly let go of my obsession with an outcome I may be pursuing, I find that results start to manifest quickly and effortlessly. In fact, at times the harder I try to achieve a goal, I find myself further from it and even blocked from reaching that destination.

The biggest case in point that elucidates this phenomenon is that each year when I attend a residential meditation retreat and am consciously cut-off from the outside world and deeply focused on my practice of Vipassana, I return home to find that many of my most complex and inscrutable challenges have resolved themselves in my physical absence. Furthermore, in many instances I find that others whom I work with and want to help mentor and develop in their professional or personal journey have stepped-up to face situations that I would typically be called upon to assist with. So not only does this have the benefit of automatic resolution relative to any direct effort I would have made, it has the side benefit of raising the confidence in others who otherwise rely on me in certain ways.

To illustrate further with a personal example, I had been coaching my daughter to play squash, a sport I enjoy, and she is inspired by the idea of learning it too. Over a year plus of weekly practice I had also been constantly urging her to seek professional coaching, which ought to have become an even easier sell when the new head coach of our sports club turned out to be a woman. Knowing my daughter looks up to and seeks out female role models in many aspects of her life, I thought my job of convincing her was about to become easier. However, despite months of insisting and even trying to create spontaneous meeting opportunities with this new pro, my headstrong child only wanted to hit the ball with her dad. So when I returned from my ten-day Vipassana retreat to the news that she had taken her first lesson with the coach while I was away as my wife had managed to convince her to give it a trial so as not to miss her weekly training routine, I could only smile in admiration of how the universe had gifted me with the blessing at a time that I was making the least conscious effort to derive this outcome. What's more, this wasn't even a goal I had thought achievable given the prior resistance.

Another spontaneous resolution, this one more in a professional context, where I was preparing myself to have a courageous conversation with a peer at work upon my return from retreat. I planned to ask them to take the reins more firmly on an important assignment that we were collaborating on for months, as the stakes were very high for all of us involved. Despite repeated hints, I had failed to get my colleague's attention and commitment over a several week period. I returned to find out that a mini-crisis had ensued at the client in question while I was away and my partner colleague had not only done an amazing job of averting the challenge on our collective behalf, but was now also feeling more energized by the prospect of leading from the front. Problem solved!

There are countless such examples that amuse me now as they are no longer surprises. My explanation, if there is one that's even possible, is that when I am working hard to remove the inner impurities in my mind through meditation instead of focusing outwardly through worldly action (which is necessary but often insufficient), the universe starts gifting me with outward solutions and outcomes that I was otherwise unable to achieve

I have finally understood and experienced the wisdom in Martin Luther King Jr.'s quote, "I have so much to do today, I'll need to spend another hour on my knees." Letting go and focusing inward while pursuing noble objectives is an essential ingredient to "receiving" in our lives.

Inner Purification Leads to Outer Alignment, p.109

Personal Reflections

Optimism in Impermanence

Once the law of impermanence (the inherently changing nature of all phenomena) is sufficiently ingrained in our mind, the wisdom arises that challenging situations cannot and will not last forever. This leaves us with a sense of optimism and relief even as we are facing difficulties.

Yes, reminders on impermanence can also be helpful when we are on the upward side of the cycle, though most people tend to not be bothered with what comes next when they are receiving a festive bounty and only when the cycle turns downward does the realization occur that nothing lasts forever.

I now try to ascribe greater positive association to the cycle of impermanence during inevitable decline in all worldly matters. When one is experiencing gains, at least that aspect itself is fulfilling. And when the dissatisfaction follows as the down cycle begins, there is a clear case for optimism because things are bound to eventually get better given their inherent cyclicality.

Just as when the sun sets each evening, we sleep with the security that it will rise again and herald the morning of the following day without fail or delay, so does the believer in the law of impermanence not doubt for a moment that (positive) change is around the corner when the outlook of a given situation looks bleak and dark at a particular time.

Just as the gardener who plants a sapling and nourishes it with adequate irrigation and access to the sun and atmosphere does so with the confidence that it will gradually grow into a sturdy tree one day, so does the student of all natural phenomena not lament the pace of change when a given circumstance seems challenging for longer than a desired period of time.

Impermanence is in action all around us if we look closely—from within the tiniest of atomic matter to the unmistakable movement in the surface of tidal waves.

All these natural phenomena remind us of their changing nature and temporariness through their very manifestation itself—changing seasons, flowers blooming, clouds shedding rain, ice caps melting into streams, rivers following gravity into lakes and oceans—and so the cycles continue incessantly forever.

Change Is Good, Change Is Inevitable, p.75
Change Is Hard, Change Is Easy, p.79

Personal Reflections

Everything Is Perfectly Timed…
…Nothing Happens Out of Order

Time and again, I now smile at the elegance with which the incidents in my life unfold as if following a perfectly designed temporal map, where each step is carefully sequenced and timed to perfection.

So many times in the past, I had wrestled with achieving a certain result by a certain time frame and driven myself and others around me anxious till the said outcome was realized, or it became completely clear that it couldn't or wouldn't be achieved. Now that I look back at those episodes, I realize that no matter what I did then or could have done differently with the benefit of hindsight, the resultant change would only have occurred if there was perfect alignment of outward effort with inner readiness and ripened environment.

On the other end of this spectrum, too often in my current life I stand back in astonishment when things seemingly occur at lightning speed with little or no overt effort on my part, as though there is some higher-order machinery that is operating on its own volition for my benefit. At times, I haven't even devised a goal or an approach to achieving a goal yet results start appearing in abundance and of higher quality than what I would have desired, and with the least possible resistance from the universe.

That such developments fill me with rapture is no surprise and have also helped me take in stride when the roadblocks also appear as spontaneously, with great intensity, and without explanation or warning. Piecing all these together over a long period of time, I can say with complete authenticity that there isn't one instance (even now as I look back) that I wish would have played out differently. I had already begun to appreciate that everything happens for a reason when I first started meditating and now have further realized that everything also happens when the time for it is perfect—no sooner or later.

Why might this be the case?

Naturally, we never question when good things happen to us, whether undeservingly or suddenly. It is when either good things take too long to manifest or seemingly bad things start to happen without anticipation that we become distraught.

My experiential explanation is that certain good things are accurately and appropriately withheld from us until such time that we are in a position to either appreciate or benefit from them. In the case of such things never manifesting, it is actually because we lack the wisdom to realize that these aren't really things that are beneficial for us or will aid in our inner development, including such desires that when fulfilled will mostly serve to boost our ego in harmful ways.

Seemingly adverse things appearing in abundance and without warning could be arising for one of two reasons. First, it may simply be that dealing with them is a necessary step in our development and without them our life journey will be a superficial success. Relatedly and importantly, these circumstances appear because prior volitional activity or accumulated karma making them the birth child of thoughts or actions we have taken in the past, whether we can directly recall or correlate to the present incidents.

Whatever the specific reason, I take great comfort in the fact that there is zero randomness in how my life's events unroll and I look ahead with optimism and enthusiasm, knowing that the temporal map of these occurrences is accurately following the karmic load that I carry and strive to purify.

No Coincidences (Or Karmic Connections), p.7
People Come into Our Lives for a Reason, p.39
Dhamma Willing, p.47
Beget Merit, Avoid Regret, p.185

Personal Reflections

Power in Acceptance

The word acceptance refers to the act of consenting to receive something that is offered or the favorable reception or approval of something or someone. The slight connotation that has come about in the typical use of the word is that of a sense of unwilling or inevitable surrender, sometimes in an undesirable or unwelcoming manner. While that needn't be the case in general, I generally see great power and merit in orienting and maintaining an acceptance mindset towards all of life's developments.

Before we delve into the deeper wisdom ingrained in this vignette, it would be easy to conclude even at the mundane level that what arises with non-acceptance is a range of unwholesome emotions like anger, resentment, fear, envy, and greed. And while nothing stops us from repurposing and channeling these negative tendencies towards achievement of objectives that remain yet unattained or unachievable, we can be guaranteed that even that effort will come with a certain degree of stress, anxiety, or agitation that will be apparent to us or, at a minimum, embodied at an unconscious level.

As such, even if wanting to continue pursuing our desired goals, denying or fighting reality can be a harmful entry point into the remaining effort with which we can yet make a difference to a given situation. The real power that stems from true acceptance and non-resistance to the challenging prompts we receive, which we may perceive as obstacles, is that by aligning our intent, energy, and orientation with the universe's guidance, direction, and blueprint, things actually start happening more spontaneously and at the optimal time.

And when they don't manifest naturally (whether to an extent or altogether), we *know* (and not just believe blindly) that there is no hidden conspiracy against us, it's simply our prior karma coming up in ways that are keeping us from the immediate prospect we desire.

So, I now feel more empowered and not stymied when I acceptingly welcome the vicissitudes of life.

Everything Is Perfectly Timed…, p.19
Kamma Vipaka - Actions Beget Outcomes, p.31
Dhamma Willing, p.47
See the Job, Do the Job, Stay Out of the Misery, p.59
The Tripod of Life, p.157
Non-Linearity of Life, p.173

Personal Reflections

No Mud, No Lotus

I was first introduced to this powerful phrase by a close friend on the same spiritual path. As an aside, in our tradition we refer to such friends as *kalyan mitra* or well-wishing friend. The role one plays is to encourage and inspire each other to continue making progress on the path.

I remember precisely how he spontaneously quipped "no mud, no lotus" when I was lamenting some challenges and setbacks in maintaining the purity of my practice (both on and off the cushion) when operating in an intense business and social context where the forces of greed, fear, and ego were too strong to avoid getting knocked down by them from time to time.

The ease and brilliance with which this gem lifted up my spirits in that moment is still vivid in my mind. And thinking of it in similar times of strain serves as a good reminder that it is far more difficult and much more commendable to stand tall when there are opposing forces trying to pull us down.

For us to make worthy progress on the inner path, we *must* overcome necessary obstacles, which are always trying to topple us when we try to make positive strides towards purity. Without such grist for the mill, we simply cannot grow as individuals.

The more nuanced and profound implication of this statement is a bit more stark and dramatic, which is that purity can only really shine in an environment that is surrounded by impurity, just like a lotus blossoms over a muddy swamp.

And it's the composition of the mud that provides for the fertile environment for the serene flower to flourish.

In his book by the same title, the renowned philosopher monk Thich Nhat Hanh implores us that the true secret to lasting happiness is to acknowledge and transform suffering by working through it and not by running away from it.

Another correlate of this insight is the knowledge that struggle and recovery go hand in hand with spiritual growth. So much so that at one point a trusted senior teacher and author in our tradition of meditation reminded me that if we encounter someone who claims to have advanced on the path towards inner purification without any outward struggle, that person is deluding either oneself or others.

Even the Buddha had to go through meaningful challenges both before and after he attained full enlightenment. It is an encouraging reminder to pick ourselves up when we are down on ourselves or when setbacks seem to derail us, that there is growth in working through these vicissitudes. To more fully and deeply root ourselves in our contemplative practice is the only way forward in such circumstances.

A cliched Urdu couplet popular in India sums it up in another visual metaphor which translates into English as, "It is an ocean of fire (reference to suffering) and I must swim across it to the other shore."

No mud, no lotus!

Inner Purification Leads to Outer Alignment, p.109

Personal Reflections

Kamma Vipaka – Actions Beget Outcomes

Kamma is the Pali word, the Hindi equivalent of which, *karma*, is now well ensconced in the English language and part of the lexicon of many people. The simplest presentation of its essence being that one's actions have meaning and consequences—whether good or bad ones—and they catch up to us, proportionally in favorable or unfavorable ways, whether we believe in taking responsibility for them or not. Often, when something untoward happens in one's own or someone else's life, we reflectively or cynically say, "it's karma", and typically elaborate or correlate it with something the individual may have done some time ago to deserve the (unfavorable) outcome.

Vipaka means result or outcome in Pali. Taken together, *kamma vipaka*, essentially conveys the notion that one's actions and their resultant outcomes go hand in hand and are in fact linked inextricably. And while most commonplace usage of karma being a lamentation about adverse outcomes stemming from past misdeeds, few amongst us focus on the corollary about meritorious deeds leading to positive future gains.

I know many people question the validity of this principle because they don't see the manifestation of it or they see enough counter-examples in their own or others' lives to buy into the ideology. I often hear illustrations like, "this colleague of mine is always getting promoted into greater responsibility despite being an unkind supervisor." On the other hand, "this person I know is always looking out for everyone and somehow never gets any recognition for it."

Whether in career, heath, or relationships, we will always have doubts about whether our actions have a direct impact on our life outcomes. Or is it that life is a series of random occurrences, and one shouldn't thus put too much credence into causality behind outcomes? It would certainly be easier to operate life in a carefree manner, unconcerned about the responsibility of causation. It can also feel depressing to believe that "the sins of the past" are always looming to cause agony in present life or some time into the future.

Years of meditation and careful observation of some of the more obvious and intuitive connections has strengthened my view that even the littlest action we take has a resultant consequence. This could seem like a yoke to bear at all times and cause us to be extra vigilant in all of our mental, physical, and vocal actions.

In reality, if you start living into this ideology, it is actually anything but that and in fact the most liberating aspect of it is the quiet confidence one can have that once I take appropriate action, the natural and proportional outcome *will* follow, whether immediately or in some cases, far into the future. So, one can actually be truly free of care or concern because we have placed our trust in the inviolable principle of *kamma vipaka.*

I can relate countless examples from my own life to illustrate the validity of this principle but instead would invite the reader to closely examine their day to day lives to see if they pick up any instances that affirm a belief in it. And when you come across a seeming contradiction to it (as you very well might), sit with it for a while, and allow the situation to fully manifest and for time and nature to take their own course.

The only friendly caution I would offer in conclusion is to be somewhat pragmatic about your approach. Given the novice stage of inner development that most of us find ourselves in, let's not expect 100% adherence in being able to guard our every action with perfection. However, with noble intention and vigilant observation, we can aim towards ensuring that sufficient thought goes into our every action so we may inherit the fruits of our merits in the future.

Inner Purification Leads to Outer Alignment, p.109
Beget Merit, Avoid Regret, p.185

Personal Reflections

Strive to Serve and Surrender

This gem emerged in a recent silent meditation retreat as my mind was subconsciously attempting to resolve a complex paradox of wanting to achieve certain life goals to fulfill my worldly obligations as a family man and career objectives as a high-achieving professional against a seemingly counter volition to avoid grasping and craving for external pursuits to create more happiness and contentment.

The desire to strive for outward results in the mundane material realm was clearly appearing at odds with aspiring for minimalism to advance in the supra-mundane spiritual realm.

It occurred to me in a rather "eureka!" sort of manner that the inner struggle was being caused by trying to solve *my* goals. If I replaced the obsession for solving for *my* needs (or wants, as the case might be), and redirected my efforts to the service of others, the struggle disappeared almost instantaneously.

What's more, it became clear that even this striving ought to be done up to a certain point and without overdue strain. Done with ease and in fact a sense of surrender after making adequate effort was the best way to keep the mind at peace and in harmony with the will and wisdom of the universe.

In essence the insights from this gem are two-fold. First, it's a lot easier and nobler when your efforts serve a greater cause (or people) beyond simply satisfying your own agenda. Second, doing so from a stance of humility and sufficiency will lead to ease and acceptance of all resultant outcomes.

From the moment this insight became self-evident, I went back through time to examine other instances where I had to struggle to align my efforts with selfless orientation or was unable to make the right effort because the objective itself was muddled or appeared to be in conflict with some other constraint.

In each instance when I conducted a thought experiment to adjust some conditionality to reorient my efforts or volition towards selfless service to others or a higher calling, I found the fog of confusion, indecision, or inaction lifting and giving me confidence that striving to serve and then surrendering can unlock simple solutions when confronted with presumably unsolvable dilemmas.

All Outcomes Are (Good) Outcomes, p.105
Inner Purification Leads to Outer Alignment, p.109

Personal Reflections

People Come into Our Lives for a Reason…
…to Bring Us Joy or to be Our Teacher

This insight might sound like a mouthful but follows the simple tenet that everything happens for a reason. As such, when people appear in our life's sphere, it is typically to either bring us joy or to be our teacher.

Let me clarify what I mean by this and how it manifests at a mundane and karmic level.

The first part is likely easy to follow and accept as it has a positive connotation. We rejoice in the company of friends, family we relish, and like-minded people from aspects of our life that give us meaning. It is said that we can choose our friends but not our parents. Whenever possible, we selectively associate ourselves with people who bring us joy, and interestingly these individuals appear in our life frame with that very karmic spirit in mind, given the simpatico kinship we experience in their enjoyable company.

The reciprocal aspect of this emergence requires a bit more elaboration and reasoning. As often (if not more often) as the individuals who bring us joy, we find others entering our lives in uninvited ways that challenge us or bring us apparent hardship. We consider these people our adversaries at worst and annoyances at best, when in fact they too are our friends that have been brought into our lives to aid (or test) our inner development in specific aspects if we can come to see it in that manner and accept it as such. The purpose these individuals fulfill in our journey is to become our teachers in aspects of our life where we are yet underdeveloped or simply blocked from potential advancement, whether we may realize it or not.

Let me illustrate this with a personal example. In my line of work, it is essential to work closely with and collaborate with peers who complement my abilities to meet the expectations of a given client executive in a satisfactory manner. There are enough times when one is unable to exercise complete personal choice in whom to partner with as many factors go into that decision.

Often enough, I must find a way to get along with individuals who may not share my ideologies and value system, which can easily lead to strain and friction. And yet, when I dig deeper, I *always* conclude that everyone has good intentions and any strain I am experiencing is either because they have a different approach to client service or developing our people, and not that they are inherently unlikable or incompatible. Abraham Lincoln summed up this insight beautifully in saying, "I don't like that man. I must get to know him better."

The implication being that when we put our guards up when seemingly adversarial people appear in our lives, it is simply because we haven't taken enough time to understand their ideologies and in fact the primary fault we find in them is that they don't perfectly conform to *our* preferred style. And if we tune into what they have to offer, it expands our horizons and we learn something new and beneficial if we maintain an open enough mind and welcoming mindset.

In essence, these people come into our lives and become our teachers in various aspects of our existence that we have consciously or unconsciously blocked off. We typically dismiss such people and quickly start scheming ways to rid ourselves of them before we have had the opportunity to learn from their varying opinions and other apparent dissimilarities we experience in them.

However, Dhamma has its own system of ensuring our inner development and we will find that there are times when despite our valiant efforts to ward off such individuals or try to banish them completely from our lives, they don't easily disappear. At this point, we either have the choice to keep fighting this development with all our might or to actually accept it as the universe's will and tune into the remedial aspects of this occurrence.

These teachers represent the only means through which we will imbibe some important and essential learning and thus are equally valuable (if not more) as are our joy-giving friends and other like-minded people, whose welcome entry into our lives we rarely question and always take for granted.

No Coincidences (Or Karmic Connections), p.7
Open to Possibility…, p.143

Personal Reflections

The Universe Provides (For My Every Need)

As I embrace the conception and realization of non-self through the internalization of impermanence of my mind and body, aside from the benefit of not taking myself quite so seriously all the time, a sudden and liberating feeling that the universe provides for my every *need* has emerged.

I now feel confident that this must be so because after all, I am but a part of the universe and furthermore, am now trying to live my life in harmony with the code of conduct designed to align oneself with it.

This is only a recent development and not something that arose immediately when I first baby-stepped onto the noble path. Unsettling as it may seem, the idea that I don't exist in distinct isolation with the rest of the universe also comes with the freedom that, as its offspring, my needs are essential for it to fulfill, especially if my conduct is in accordance with its principles.

Just like no parent willingly or knowingly allows their children to go without all their necessities—food, education, clothes, medicine, supplies, friends—so does the universe attend to my every essential need. And even though an ordinary parent may have limitations due to the extent of their means (although that too is limitless should they be in alignment with the universe), here the vast and all-powerful universe has boundless capacity to care for me in every manner it deems appropriate and necessary.

Even as this insight started to crystallize slowly but clearly in my mind during recent years, I didn't want to just accept it without testing its potency. And now having done so on many an occasion, I have found that if two conditions are in place, the formula operates with scientific precision.

First, the concept applies to *needs* and not *wants* and the universe is quite discerning as to which is which, even if *I* might try to rationalize some wants as needs. In other words, the universe only provides something (or anything) to the extent that it is truly an essentiality that I cannot live without at the material level, for my inner development on the path, or for my ability to serve others.

I could provide countless examples to demonstrate this principle but the most powerful and profound one is how year after year, the space, time, and support has appeared for me to participate in a residential meditation retreat even when the most challenging of situations at work or home seem to threaten the prospect. And this comes about without abandoning any other life priority but in harmony with all the associated circumstances, each and every time.

Another validation of this principle is the increasing confidence and security I feel about my ability to provide for my family and discharge all my duties as a householder even as I orient a portion of my time towards a life of service and intend to do so with increasingly greater capacity in alignment with the self-prescribed stages of life.

Embodying this life plan brings me to the second condition for this principle to do its work. Much like a dependent child does relative to their providing parent, we must truly let go and believe that our needs are going to be met if we continue to do our part by way of putting in the right effort.

To be sure, this is not meant to imply passivism or sitting with one hand on top of another and waiting for everything to fall into your lap from the universe. It means to pursue what you must at the mundane level but do so with a detached mind that is free from anxiety induced by craving and thus remaining fully available to receive the support from the universe that makes your efforts materialize into the requisite level of output.

This gem is best enjoyed directly through firsthand realization and also with a great deal of patience as it is not most intuitively obvious and yet, potent and liberating.

See the Job, Do the Job, Stay Out of the Misery, p.59
Galloping Wants Outpace Needs, p.127
The Other Quadrants of Life, p.179

PERSONAL REFLECTIONS

Dhamma Willing

Dhamma willing as a notion is naturally a play on the more well-known and frequently used phrases like "God willing" or "Inshallah." These and countless other similar legislates imply that instead of tossing and turning in times of great difficulty or dilemma, it's optimal to surrender to some higher power that we trust or respect as a general maxim to living a stress-free life.

While I truthfully haven't given a great deal of specific thought to what I now feel about a certain concept of God as I may have in the past, I do have a relatively clear conception of the essential universal principles I now espouse and believe underpin the plane of existence that I exist within. And for all practical purposes, this is as much understanding I need in order to progress in my life with peace and equanimity.

Some of these tenets include a realization that as soon as I allow any mental defilements to arise in my mind—be that greed, fear, anger, envy, or lust—I immediately suffer a dose of anxiety. Contrarily, when I remain at ease with my circumstances, or better yet, generate love and goodwill for those around me, I am gifted with a prompt reward of inner peace and happiness.

And these two principles can only really be appreciated through direct knowledge and experience of impermanence (or non-constancy) in all phenomena. In simple terms, any situation—whether seemingly good or bad—is always in the process of changing, which thus helps us appreciate that it is pointless to lament unfavorable circumstances and equally futile to expect that a favorable moment will last forever. In other words, change truly is the only constant in all aspects of life—however big or small—and nothing is really in place forever—whether a person, place, or feeling.

Another key construct that has affirmed itself is that the source of mental defilements, which in turn cause misery, is directly dependent on how much I entangle myself with likes (wants), dislikes (avoidances), and self-orientation (egotism).

And the readily available countermeasure to maintain a peaceful orientation is an active cultivation of equanimity at all times. This, in turn, can be done through a conscious and constant choice to simply observe and not blindly react to external stimuli. These imposing inputs directly manifest as mental formations and physical sensations within the framework of my mind and body and can be neutralized through Vipassana meditation.

What has also become very clear is that when I live my life conforming to these universal principles of nature (or Dhamma), I find that my actions and circumstances start to improve spontaneously or at the very least my ability to deal with situations is considerably improved even when there is adversity. Correspondingly, when I act in defiance of these simple and timeless truths, I am bereft of the ability to deal with challenges and the outcomes resulting from my actions remain unfavorable.

I have also concluded through close examination that there is no gimmick or irrationality or inexplicability associated with the linkage between my mental, physical, and verbal actions with outcomes that arise from them. Aside from aspects of life that I don't directly control, like the proverbial hand I may have been dealt, I can only control my direct efforts and must contend with a given starting point that I don't control (or at best, can only indirectly influence). Just like we don't question the existence of gravity in the universe and see it manifest in all physical phenomenon, so it is with Dhamma manifesting in all aspects of our existence with certain mathematical precision.

There are times when I can easily draw the direct connection between my actions and the resultant outcomes after accounting for extraneous factors that I don't control, be it actions of other individuals, or macro-events that can impact humanity at large. However, when I am unable to see the connection with my limited abilities, I live in the confident comfort that because I have acted or generated a noble volition in accordance with Dhamma, the derivative outcomes will always be good, whatever they maybe (even if this is not immediately apparent). And if they are not, there must be a deeper karmic reason that I am unable to comprehend at the time of taking the action and will become self-evident in the future.

To be sure, this isn't some blind-faith approach akin to complete and unquestioning surrender to some super-being. In fact, it is the logical conclusion of an inherently inquisitive and scientifically trained mind that only believes what it has been able to bear out through actual, rational and direct personal experience. And having thus studied countless situations—from the past and in the present—with varying level of actions on my part and drawing relevant correlates, have concluded that Dhamma acts with as much certainty as does gravity.

My leadership coach summed it up very practically when I shared this emergence with him during a session by thus concluding in plain English, "Things always work out in the mind. And if they haven't worked out, it must not yet be the end!" Thus, I fearlessly and confidently keep progressing on the path in the knowledge that things always work out in the end if I keep doing my part—Dhamma willing!

Inner Purification Leads to Outer Alignment, p.109
The Tripod of Life, p.157

Personal Reflections

UNCOMMON COMMONSENSE

Seeing Is Believing

One of the underlying principles of Vipassana (or insight) meditation is that we only truly believe and internalize phenomenon that we actually observe within the framework of our own mind and body. Said differently, the only reality that is meaningful and beneficial to us is the one we experience firsthand without having to infer anything indirectly through either intellectual reasoning or unquestioned blind faith in wisdom expounded by others we trust or respect.

This tenet appeals to me greatly as I have always believed in experiential or deduced learning over taking the written word or narrated testimonials as gospel, be it in mundane outward aspects or in the context of inner personal development.

This commonly known insight is offered here with two-fold appeal, which might seem contradictory on the surface.

First, I have found every step of the way that every firsthand learning has truly left (and continues to leave) an indelible mark on my mind. I find myself internalizing (and thus following diligently) lifestyle changes or new mindsets, more fully and completely.

The most dramatic change in the mind-body context, having been a fond and frequent consumer of alcohol for most of my adult life, was the sudden decision and irrevocable commitment to abstain from it completely and permanently. Once the inner realization that any form of intoxication was detrimental to cultivating equanimity distinctly arose in my mind while getting introduced to Vipassana meditation, I needed no further reminders to accept and maintain this lifestyle and social reset.

There are countless such epiphanies that have arisen and have become easy to embrace as principles of my ongoing existence, be they personal, professional, or relational in nature.

The second aspect of this gem I offer may seem to be a contradiction to the purpose of this book. Only believe as much as you can observe and accept firsthand. These stories and ideas are written with an intent to stir inspiration through relatability of lived experiences and not meant as recommended beliefs to follow without direct confirmation and trial.

Ehipassiko – Come, See for Yourself!, p.135

Personal Reflections

See the Job, Do the Job, Stay Out of the Misery

This well-known quote from Maharishi Mahesh Yogi sums up its wisdom in few words and is self-explanatory. Yet, let me yet offer some elaboration and personal corroboration.

The primary essence of it is simply that we must focus on the task at hand or the role we are required to play, do our level best at it, then forget about the result. Whatever result, seemingly good or bad, will be what it will be anyway, and getting hassled about it when we are making the effort will only serve to diminish the effort itself or worsen the outcome.

Obsessing over the outcome introduces anxiety and insecurity into our minds. Naturally, our efforts must be directed towards a specific goal but not in such a manner that if that goal isn't achieved, our effort is not worthwhile. The irony is that obsessing over outcomes simply serves to reduce the likelihood of the outcome being beneficial.

Another source of misery stems from thought processes such as, "What's in it for me?" or "What effort will be of foremost value to me?", and thus we either don't make the requisite effort (when we can't determine a clear self-oriented angle) or we do so in a manner that is personal agenda-oriented. When self-orientation is attached to the goal or to our efforts, it induces even greater anxiety in us, which doesn't go away when the apparent objective is met because another such cycle of grasping and attachment ensues in some other context.

The beauty of the embodiment of this counsel in our day-to-day lives is that it actually enhances our ability to derive results in a wholesome and anxiety-free manner. As such, we either achieve the desired outcome from our efforts or develop the ability to face an adverse outcome in a peaceful and accepting manner.

The Tripod of Life, p.157

PERSONAL REFLECTIONS

No Free Lunch

As in any other aspect of our lives, the idea that what you put into your meditation practice (or life in general) is what you get out of it. Having made the case for prioritizing meditation as an essential ingredient in one's inner development, one must also appreciate the relative proportionality of one's effort to the resultant impact.

Expecting miracles from meditation while not practicing consistently or putting requisite time into it is a folly. Having said that, a little goes a long way and even committing modest efforts towards a daily practice can yield wonders over time. What's more, once you make that commitment and treat it like any other life habit that you take for granted or deem essential like eating, bathing, sleeping, or exercising, you will also find that the universe starts to come to your assistance and enables you to follow through on that promise.

When I first started practicing, I was fearful that my hectic lifestyle, which included near-daily travel, would derail my ability to sustain any regularity and continuity. But I quickly found creative ways to maintain my commitment by learning to meditate in atypical settings like the seat of an airplane, the backseat of a taxi, or in the seclusion of a hotel room. All sorts of supportive forces came to my aid as soon as I started to take baby steps towards a cause that is rooted in a noble volition of the mind.

I have similarly discovered that incorporating one annual retreat, which seemed completely formidable to accommodate given the effort required to attend the first introductory course, has become relatively easy to sustain with support from my family, colleagues, and clients. I am grateful that circumstances always mysteriously conspire in my favor when I resolve to maintain my strong determination to uphold this yearly commitment.

I don't take for granted the fact that I must put in the time and effort towards sustaining my practice and getting further established on the path in order to sustain the associated benefits. The notion that "there's no free lunch" also holds true in the inner realm of meditation as much as it does in the outer world of materiality!

Personal Reflections

Binge Eating Causes Tummy Trouble

Just as there is no free lunch in the world of spiritual growth, I find that the other extreme of "binging" on meditation, especially when it comes at the expense of other priorities in life, can lead to other sorts of challenges. Most of us don't have the luxury (or renunciation orientation) of being a full-time monk or nun, who can devote their entire life, and each waking minute, either towards their own spiritual development or in service to others on a similar path. As such, practicing meditation in a manner that runs counter to upholding our roles as householders with worldly responsibilities can become a form of escape and, at worst, can alienate people or priorities that matter to us.

I can well appreciate the temptation to go headlong into one's practice, especially when we experience strong initial and ongoing benefits, and put the rest of our responsibilities on hold. While this may be acceptable for a period of time to create an impactful imprint of the meditation technique on our inner minds, if this is done in part to consciously or unconsciously escape from life's challenges, it isn't something that will be beneficial to us in the long run. A healthy practice of meditation is one that integrates naturally into the routine of our mainstream activities, until such time when life's circumstances organically allow us to advance further towards it.

In fact, it can have the benefit of impacting other aspects of life in a positive manner be it through sharpening one's focus and ability to be more productive or achieving a more neutral acceptance of challenging situations, allowing the mind to remain balanced and coolly move ahead in the right direction, recognizing what is in our control and what is not.

I have been fortunate in this regard as starting from my first introductory course where I experienced profound benefits from learning meditation, my conducting teacher picked up on my inherent tendency to go to extremes and cautioned me immediately to follow the middle way in this aspect of spiritual development. I am also fortunate that my wife, who is wholly supportive of my journey on the path and was also the initial impetus in its direction, also serves as an important check and balance. She reminds me when I am devoting too much time towards meditation and related activities, especially on weekends, interfering with my priority to spend quality time with my family.

I have also found that our inner mind actually possesses the wisdom to know when we are off-centered in this regard and signals us to strike the right balance. It is up to us to heed its counsel and manage our outward professional and personal commitments in the service of society and family alongside the pursuit of inner development. What is also compelling about taking this balanced approach is that the true test of inner peace is our ability to sustain it in the real world of society and adversaries and not only in the serene environment of a meditation center surrounded by like-minded fellow seekers on the path.

The Mahatma Gandhi was a *mahatma* (great soul) because he was able to bring his posture and practice of non-violence, cultivated over years of inner training, into the real world, facing adversity from his oppressors while charting out a path towards salvation for himself and his fellow countrymen.

Seductive as it may be to plunge into a full-time practice of meditation, I urge fellow serious meditators to consider the unintended impact of creating and perpetuating a misimpression that meditation is only really suitable for yogis, hippies, or escapists.

Personal Reflections

Comfort with Discomfort

The primary aspect of observing one's mind and body during meditation in a choiceless and observational manner has an important implication for how we spend the rest of our time and how we conduct ourselves in general.

The essence of choicelessness and mere observation is that we consciously opt not to react to how we are feeling—physically or mentally—during the period of meditation. What arises during meditation are thoughts, emotions, and bodily sensations ranging from pleasant, neutral, to unpleasant in nature. Even if one hasn't learned to meditate yet, it would be easy to accept the premise that both pleasant and neutral thoughts and physical sensations don't bring us apparent agony and are easy to observe, process, and accept.

It is when we experience mental or physical discomfort while meditating that the mind and body will urge us to react and get rid of the cause of the unease. However, it is our vow and choice to not react during the meditative practice and this is what enables the building of equanimity (in small yet powerful doses) and leads to the cultivation of inner peace.

The beauty of this mind training process is that we start building the ability to be comfortable with discomfort, even while not meditating, which is how we spend most of our time. Even superficial reminders not to be thrown off balance when external perturbations occur can be a helpful aid.

Much like the athlete who invests hours in training for a marathon, building up the stamina, muscle memory, mental strength, and sheer endurance to stay the course on race-day (which can come with known and unknown surprises like positive group effect and adrenalin high and negative unexpected rough weather or a head cold), so does a meditator build confidence that life's ups and downs can be dealt with through equanimity developed during hours in meditation.

And even as an athlete can hit a pothole, lose their stride and then get back into rhythm, so can the meditator lose their footing through life's stumbles and bounce back with agility and resilience.

Personal Reflections

Change Is Good, Change Is Inevitable

It is believed that the ancient Greek philosopher, Heraclitus, brought forward the powerful insight, "The only constant in life is change," which is typically referred to in the condensed and reversed form, "Change is the only constant." Comparing existential things to the flow of a river, he goes on to say that you could not step twice into the same river if taking a dip.

The wisdom in this quote is timeless, universal, liberating, and sometimes unsettling. We relish change when circumstances improve for the better and don't question why they came about naturally. And yet, most of us struggle with change when it is undesirable or when we believe it is negative or unfavorable.

The deeper insight that has surfaced over the years of practicing meditation is that not only is change inevitable, it is truly essential. Why do I now believe in the essentiality of change?

Change represents the rhythm of life—what is born must grow and then decay and eventually pass away. Change also confirms that our actions have outcomes—be they ones we aim for or not.

Change occurs every moment at the most minuscule level of all molecular matter. Our mind is unable to witness this level of incessant and subtle change and contents itself with observing the gross reality of existence where things *appear* to remain the same.

But as the astute observation from Heraclitus reminds us, even two consecutive dips in flowing water are not taken in the same river. How many of us, on a daily basis, are dealing with changes in our circumstances and wondering why they don't comply to our wish of remaining constant?

Considering change as essential respects the continuity and fluidity of life. If there were no change, winter would not herald spring, nor would children spring out of wombs. The contrarian might ask about the value or discomfort of change that ushers in the cold winter after the temperate autumn, or the suffering and sickness and eventually death that comes with aging. While that type of change may seem negative, it is an essential rhythm of life. Things need to decay and die for new things to come in their place.

Imagine a world where nothing would ever extinguish? Destruction and creation are two sides of the same coin. One cannot exist without the other. As a practical matter, the planet would be overrun if there was infinite extension of life. Children would be overwhelmed with the burden of the aging. The elderly would suffer endlessly from sickness.

If one works back from these foretelling possibilities, it would be easy to conclude that even seemingly "negative" change—towards decay or destruction—is both essential and eventually beneficial. One journey must complete for a new one to begin.

Personal Reflections

Change Is Hard, Change Is Easy

Despite the constancy of change, most of us struggle with it, and rarely welcome it with open arms unless truly stuck in a rut and the only way out is something different. We are all creatures of habit and the simple-minded reason for not seeking or embracing change is that it typically disrupts a comfortable routine or rhythm.

Simple things like trying out a new restaurant or even a different meal option at the same neighborhood joint we frequent, comes with some trepidation of potential dissatisfaction.

There is comfort, efficiency, loyalty, and even anticipatory nostalgia in familiarity of choices, people, places, and routines. So, when a new development appears on the horizon, we view it as a threat to our self-created illusion of permanence. We often resist inevitable change with every bone in our bodies, longing for the past or present to linger on.

We offer rationale for this sentiment depending on the circumstances. Sometimes we justify averting change to save ourselves the effort or mental reorientation to adjust to a new context. Sometimes we continue living in circumstances, afflicted by habits that we know are not conducive to our wellbeing, finding ourselves paralyzed to step out of those situations even when we possess the means and the wisdom that change is necessary.

The Stockholm syndrome is an extreme example where the hostage is satisfied enough with their clearly suboptimal circumstance to befriend their own captor, who is directly responsible for creating that unfriendly or hostile situation in the first place! Fear of the unknown makes us enjoy the status quo to a fault even when we intellectually know the change to be desirable. Change feels hard.

And yet, change can and ought to be easy. Why?

For one, change is hardwired into all processes and phenomena in the universe. Resisting change is akin to wishing to make water flow uphill. Expecting change to be more gradual is asking to intentionally experience life in slow motion. Latching onto what's sure and familiar is to banish all intrigue and possibility from life.

And despite what you or I may wish, change is what literally makes the world go around and is what ensures that seasons will keep turning and children will keep growing. The sooner we can tune ourselves into the frequency of the constantly changing universe, the faster we will start flowing like a commingled stream in the confluence of conscious personal effort and the preexisting karmic conditioning.

Optimism in Impermanence, p.15
Change Is Good, Change Is Inevitable, p.75

Personal Reflections

Win Some, Lose Some, Learn Some

The commonly used phrase "win some, lose some" gets ingrained early on in life to help us put failures in perspective and build sportsman spirit when we don't succeed despite best efforts.

We are taught to "learn from failures" and not be sore losers. Interestingly, we don't often stand back and try and learn from our successes. We tend to take successes as a given or as a deserved reward for our efforts.

Somewhere between the knowledge of how suffering gets generated when we crave certain outcomes or avert others and the realization that every win or loss is a matter of relative assessment and not an absolute one, my orientation towards such seemingly binary and zero-sum outcomes is one of learning from them regardless of which side of the ledger they get accounted in.

So instead of consoling myself on failures or overly rejoicing on successes, I try re-orientating towards "what does this situation or outcome offer by way of learning?" I find this to be a more productive way of having an aggregated perspective on my effort to output. Conjoined with the insight that my effort is only one-third of what drives the outcome, I don't fret when the outcomes are not what I expected despite best (or even optimum) efforts.

This mindset more quickly allows me to move onto the next important assignment and not cause my self-worth to get wrapped-up in that adverse outcome, as I was more prone to in the past. Similarly, when I am blessed with success, I maintain the perspective that other contributory factors must have come to my aid in ensuring a favorable outcome and thus avoid falling into an egotistical trap of believing solely in my abilities as the primary driver.

All Outcomes Are (Good) Outcomes, p.105
The Tripod of Life, p.157

Personal Reflections

Prioritize People Over Projects

In the race to amassing achievements and accolades, I was often trading off people and connections in favor of "projects" and other priorities. I have now clearly concluded that the more important metric to index on is people.

As the demands of life and work continued to expand, the biggest victim was quality time spent with people, be it close family, personal friends, professional colleagues, or complete strangers simply seeking a connection and the gift of my time and attention.

Learning to meditate, including the practice of loving kindness and compassionate love towards all beings, reminded me of the essence of the proverb that my father tried to ingrain in us through childhood, "It is nice to be important but more important to be nice."

We all deal with some hopes and fears. This realization has allowed me to reset the orientation of suffering, and instead have an obligation and kinship towards the communities in which I operate and devote my time and energy to them while not neglecting my professional or householder duties.

I have also come to realize that the time I expend in cultivating relationships or assisting others actually comes back and pays disproportional positive dividends.

So, in the end, my reorientation towards people over projects hasn't resulted in any net productivity loss or reduction in direct effort towards desired output. If anything, my pursuit of these goals has become more wholesome and fulfilling.

As my sense of ego has gradually been diminishing, I fear no loss of position or profit in sharing the journey with these compatriots who magically appear as I open myself towards greater inclusivity with a people-first mindset.

By softening my singular and obsessive destination-orientation and focusing on caring about my fellow journeymen, I experience an increased sense of harmony in the context of human dynamics. When asked if friendship was perhaps half the journey, the Buddha clarified that friendship on the path is the entire path in reference to the pursuit of spiritual awakening! I find that applying that principle even in a mundane worldly context also serves me well in material ways.

Personal Reflections

Better to Fail at One's Purpose Than Succeed at Another's

As I tread the path of gaining insight into myself, another realization is that so much of what I had been doing was in pursuit of objectives and outcomes that were extrinsically defined and motivated. In essence, I was living life in service of expectations set for myself by others, whether directly or implicitly, and I had internalized these expectations and misperceived them as my own.

Meditation brought forth two-fold clarity that while there wasn't a big detriment in what I was pursuing at the mundane level, the manner in which I was striving could be reoriented to make the same pursuits much more wholesome and holistic. And if I don't pursue some of the supra-mundane aspects of my existence, I would be doing great disservice to myself and potentially even to others.

While inner demons such as self-doubt of being wrong or fear of being ridiculed often rear their heads, they are quickly overpowered by the wellspring of volition to share and pay forward the treasure I feel has been bestowed upon me. When the effort in bringing forward the message of inner purification is met with resistance or rejection, I have clarity that it would be better to fail at that objective instead of dousing the flame which is now burning brightly.

I find it no coincidence that despite the multifarious responsibilities that my life circumstances impose on me, whether as a son, a husband, a parent, or a professional, the universe keeps sending reinforcements in the form of heightened capacity and both visible and invisible helping hands for me to put greater effort into fueling the inner flame.

Personal Reflections

When in Doubt, Do the Right Thing

A fairly clear dictum that emerged during my first introduction to the practice of meditation and has increasingly become an inviolable truth is the idea that our inner mind always knows when we are about to err, and if we are in tune with it even slightly, it affords us the opportunity to make the right choice in the form of our mental, physical, or vocal actions.

Too often, we ignore, numb-out or even override this inner counsel that is actually meant for our own protection and is available to all of us and at all times. Whether dulled out or fairly developed, our conscience tries its best to keep us from harming ourselves when we are about to take steps that may harm us or others.

How does one channel this inner wisdom in the moment of truth (or strain) when other negative forces are tempting us to fray?

The signal that the mind offers is that of doubt—both in instances when we are about to do something harmful and also when we are hesitating from doing something noble. In this context, this period of indecision is actually a good thing because it allows us that extra bit of time, even if it be an infinitesimal moment, to rethink our choices. And therein lies the opportunity to pick the optimal (or at least more suitable) path.

Another way to think about this is that the reason doubt arises is to afford us the opportunity to reevaluate our choices. If we are on autopilot in a heedless manner or ready to bulldoze anything that seems to get in the way of our ill-intentioned or ignorant choices, we miss this signal at our own peril. The appearance of doubt is the flashing red-light signaling that we are about to make a suboptimal choice—whether a grave or trivial one.

I feel so grateful to have had this epiphany early enough and also the time to practice it deeply and attest to its efficacy when constantly confronted with choices—big and small—that need to be measured carefully to avoid harm to myself and others and ideally to create benefit and merit for everyone.

We frequently mistake short-term "profit" or instant gratification as a reason for overlooking this tenet and only later realize that forsaking something in the moment will not cause us to lose out in the end, even at the apparent mundane level. And even if there is some "loss" incurred in the worldly context, the deficit we might avoid at the karmic level by doing the right thing is reason enough to stay true to this moral injunction.

Follow Your Inner Compass, p.119
Begit Merit, Avoid Regret, p.185

Personal Reflections

In Sickness and In Health

This well-known idiom from the eternal vows of matrimony is something that found another meaning for me through my journey on the path of meditation. Married happily with the benefits of companionship of a spouse to comfort me in good times and bad, I find that following a spiritual path creates another eternal inner companion that won't desert me even if the worldly life partner does.

I am not referring to the notion of being married to a spiritual path or religious order as one's sole sense of belonging. I mean it in a somewhat different context.

As we commit to developing an inner practice of any kind, we discover that so much of the ups and downs in life are a matter of our relative point of view—success vs failure, gain vs loss, prestige vs disrepute, abundance vs scarcity, community vs solitude, joy vs sorrow, respect vs insult, friends vs enemies, and on and on. Even when there is hardship in the form of ill-health, poverty, physical harm, or emotional trauma, the power to disabuse ourselves of the feelings of despair lies very much in our hands, no matter the circumstances.

What's more is that the appreciation of constant change and impermanence of all universal phenomenon creates a sense of optimism because the rays of sunlight are bound to emerge at some point in the future, no matter how dark or ominous the night may be, because the laws of nature govern that daybreak must inevitably follow the night.

In the inspiring account of *Man's Search for Meaning*, Viktor Frankl describes his survival in a Nazi concentration camp by not allowing the feelings of hopelessness to set into his mind despite all external circumstances driving him in that direction by simply controlling his inner response to the outward harm his mind and body were experiencing. It is a remarkable example of the power of inner peace and how it can enable us to weather any storm on the outside if we cultivate that facility on the inside through conscious and regular contemplative practice.

Mahatma Gandhi is another fine example of a leader who practically invited physical harm and isolation in captivity to insist on, what he believed were, basic human rights and liberties. He moved an entire nation and its unwelcome British rulers by his strongly held belief in non-violent means despite being subject to hardships, reminding us that having an inner rooting provides us an eternal companion that doesn't just serve us in fair weather.

So, whether you have a devoted and loving worldly companion or not, I invite you to find your own inner guide that will be your north star that will enlighten your path even in the darkest of nights.

Personal Reflections

INSCRUTABLE MIND

All Outcomes Are (Good) Outcomes

All through life we seek to achieve and enjoy good outcomes and do our best to avoid bad ones. I have realized through my meditation that, with the exception of a handful of absolutes, all outcomes are simply outcomes and thus neither inherently good nor bad. It is the lens through which we view them that colors them favorably or unfavorably relative to our mundane life's context.

How could this possibly be true?

Let's look at something as simple and frequent as a typical exchange of goods, assets, or services between two parties who may be on opposite sides of a transaction. To illustrate, I will pick something which changes in value practically by the day, if not by the minute.

When two people trade the stock of a company in a virtual or physical marketplace or exchange, they must first come to an agreement on a suitable price. Typically, the buyer is purchasing the asset with an anticipation that the underlying value of the company is likely to rise and thus owning the stock at the price it is being offered is a decent bargain relative to future expectations.

On the other hand, the seller is thinking that the moment may be an opportune one to part with the certificate of ownership as they expect that either the company it represents is optimally valued or might even be susceptible to a price decline and thus now might be a suitable time to profit.

Can we say whether for each party the transaction represents a good or bad outcome?

I suppose it can be argued that only at a future time can we confidently say whether the buyer or the seller were more right than wrong. And yet, at the moment of transaction, each of them genuinely believes, if not hopes, that they are making the right bet and thus expecting a good outcome.

To drive the point home, if you were to look at this exchange from the standpoint of the trader, broker, or market maker, in their mind the transaction is simply a transaction and can't really be classified as good or bad.

And thus it is in life. If we view the objective facts of a situation from the standpoint of a neutral observer, we will conclude that nearly all occurrences are good outcomes and it is only when we introduce our subjective relativity, our personal agenda, that we start viewing things as good or bad.

Having examined situation upon situation I have firmly concluded that outcomes are just outcomes—neither good nor bad—and if it helps to relate to them in an evaluative manner, I would even go so far as to say that "all outcomes are good outcomes".

Personal Reflections

Inner Purification Leads to Outer Alignment

One of the most counter-intuitive and yet brilliantly simple realizations I had is that whatever is inside my mind is what manifests in my life outside.

If my mind is filled with impurities, defilements, worries, anxieties, enmities, fears, superstitions, insecurities, or foreboding, that is precisely how my external environment organizes itself and provides me validation for these mental states through my lived experiences. And on the contrary, if my mind is filled with peace, harmony, joy, friendly vibes, equanimity, compassion, or empathy then I am gifted in turn with these very conditions in the real world.

I have come to appreciate this emergence both at a mundane level and also at a karmic level. At the most fundamental level, it is easy to understand that our mental state drives the nature of our actions which typically mirror our emotions and feelings. These actions, when conceived in the womb of defilements and impurities, result in interactions with the outside world with that negative framing.

It is not hard to follow that we receive reciprocal activity in response to our actions. So, when we lead with these negative conditions, we find the same negativity being returned to (or directed toward) us, in the form of events or actions from others, that confirm our inner state of mind.

Take for instance anxiety about one's career growth. If I spend time fearing a negative outcome associated with a potential promotion for which I am being considered, I will likely misperceive actions that others are taking or I might start acting in ways that would sabotage my own success.

And with such self-sabotaging behavior, others will likely start wondering if I am deserving of the promotion in the first place, even if they were positively or neutrally disposed towards the idea in the past, which will only serve to further perpetuate the downward spiral.

On the other hand, if I focus my entire capacity on putting in my best effort toward the desired goal and not inflict myself with the anxiety associated with the future outcome, I will more likely give myself the best chance at true success.

Now let's also understand this insight through the lens of karmic energy and connections, which relates to the popularized law of attraction, that we magnetize towards us situations or people based on our thoughts. This could apply to both favorable and unfavorable thoughts which would then manifest into parallel outcomes. While the causes for this synchronicity aren't entirely evident, at a mundane level, my simple-minded understanding is along the following lines.

Essentially, in aspects pertaining to the inner mind's wavelength, like attracts like and creates resonance. In other words, our mind (or brain for those more scientifically inclined) transmits electromagnetic waves of varying frequencies. Just as in physics, when sound waves of similar frequencies come together, they create resonance or amplification of those waves.

And thus, if we are emitting waves of peace, harmony, contentment, and equanimity, these get synchronized with other energy centers—human or non-human, visible or invisible—that are also creating similar waves, leading to an intensification of our virtuous qualities. On the flip side, if I generate neurobiological activity corresponding to defilements like anger, anxiety, fear or inadequacy, these destructive qualities get amplified and magnified.

Much like intense sound waves in high resonance don't just limit themselves to the quality of producing music or cacophony, they can also shatter glass that is in its path. In other words, the waves can also create physical impact. Similarly, the brain waves when in strong resonance don't limit themselves to being mere thoughts, they can actually cause actions and situations to manifest in their accordance.

With this parallelism and link between inner thoughts and outer manifestation clear and repeatedly confirmed personally through frequent investigation and observation, it begs to reason that the purer my inner mind becomes, the better my outer circumstances will be from a karmic connection standpoint. This realization has served as another reinforcement to continue on the path to focus inward and continue the lifelong journey towards inner purification.

Time and again, I return from my meditation retreats to find that while I was away and working intently to remove certain defilements from my mind, that correspond to certain life situations associated with those conditioned complexes, their worldly correlates were also resolved!

Initially, I wondered if these apparent miracles were either figments of my creative imagination, truly random and accidental occurrences, or just temporary fixes. Having examined them deeply and identified the linkages to my inner work, they now seem rather intuitive, even if I don't have the direct ability to pick and choose what defilement gets removed at what point when I meditate!

Do Nothing and Achieve Everything…, p.11

Personal Reflections

Mind Creates Matter

Einstein expounded the theory of relativity with a brilliant postulate about the interchangeability of energy and matter that took others a long time to bear out and verify firsthand. We also hear commonsense phrases like "mind over matter" that clearly legislate that mind is the supreme and foremost entity that is primordial and precedes all other phenomenon.

Wisdom in proverbs such as, "watch your thoughts, they become words; watch your words, they become actions…", validate that the mind is the progenitor of our every choice. It also doesn't require proof that humankind, through action, creates material output through the harnessing of natural forces and resources.

These maxims and observations have melded in my mind into an insight that not only equates mind and matter and accepts their interchangeability but further states that it is the mind that actually creates matter—both consciously and unconsciously.

What does this really mean?

I think we can safely accept this premise at the mundane level if we look at simple examples like agriculture, manufacturing, or construction. Through a chain of events starting with an idea of a blueprint arising in one or more minds, we see the creation or production of physical output using a combination of naturally occurring resources, harnessed in a clever manner to seek a certain material goal.

In the karmic context, the way I understand it now is that our mind is essentially the remainder (or carry over) of unresolved karma from prior forms of existence, which we lug around with us as excess baggage from time immemorial. And even if one doesn't believe the premise of previous lives, it is not hard to accept that the originating mind is the entry point to consciousness when a being takes birth.

Even in this aspect, it is our incoming mind (albeit combined with influencing factors like external environment and personal effort) that dictates our actions, which thus result in materiality. At a further deeper level, it is the existence of a mind, any mind, that represents this unresolved karmic remainder, that forces the creation of the entity which now represents its life form moving through this universe with its incoming energy and seeking a path towards reduction (and eventual dissolution and removal) of that unresolved karma.

This powerful conclusion not only builds upon and validates the supremacy of the mind over matter, but importantly serves as a constant reminder that the path for liberation must originate and end in our mind as our every action and output is directly conceived by it.

In conclusion, it helps to understand, accept, and embody that...

Mind is matter....

Mind also becomes matter...

And importantly, it is mind that creates matter...

Personal Reflections

Follow Your Inner Compass

The basic notion of a geographic compass for direction setting doesn't require much explanation. Most readers may also be familiar with the concept of a moral compass in the context of people expressing or following their value system.

I have found over the years that my practice has built inside of me an increasingly robust, inviolable, and holistic inner compass that helps guide my every action and decision—be it trivial or monumental.

So something as uneventful as whether to take an extra helping during a meal, to how to respond to an insult, to deal with injury or disease, to disciplining my child, to major career choices, my inner compass provides for the necessary guidance without me consciously invoking its use.

Contrasting this with the past, when I would instead be dousing any moral rectitude that would arise uninvitedly as I found myself rationalizing a choice that was clearly suboptimal if not downright unethical, I now find myself cherishing and burnishing the self-directing personalized north star that keeps me from breaking my commitment to living a truthful and conscious life.

And lest anyone consider this as some self-aggrandizing statement, it actually comes from a place of humility and understanding that the moment I break (or consider breaking) any of the precepts of rightful living, I am meted out with a dose of anxiety proportional to the extent and gravity of the (potential) breakage of the moral code. This realization allows me to operate within a simple self-discovered principle that simply legislates, "when in doubt, do the right thing."

And while this internally hardwired GPS is clearly something that has built itself up in greater measure since the time I took my first baby steps on the noble path, it is actually something that inherently resides in each of us, meditator or not. It is truly up to each of us whether we choose to listen to its soft knocks on the insides of our conscience when it seeks to keep us from erring in small or big ways.

Naturally, if one starts to commit to a life of meditation and inner purification, the knocks get louder and louder and the seeker finds it impossible to ignore this inner compass' deafening roar, which is built only to provide self-protection from taking steps that will cause both mundane loss and poor karma in the future even when the choice appears superficially profitable in the near term.

When in Doubt, Do the Right Thing, p.95

Personal Reflections

Every Upset Is a Set-up in Reverse

One of my former colleagues shared this insight with me over a decade ago and demonstrated it literally by writing on a whiteboard the word UP-SET and then reversing the word fragments to express SET-UP instead. I was amused by the cleverness of the anagram-like ideology and thus the concept stayed with me over the years. Similarly, sayings like "Sweet are the uses of adversity..." or "A blessing in disguise" also convey the idea that there is long-term merit in enduring a period of challenge and have been around for quite some time.

The interesting nuance and prospective application of this insight lies in is intuiting its wisdom with foresight instead of analyzing it in hindsight. It is a lot easier to look back later when the challenge has been overcome.

What is interesting now is that when an apparently problematic situation comes about, my mind attunes itself to the possibility that this is a temporary set-back (or UP-SET) or perhaps not a set-back at all but a springboard (or SET-UP) for something valuable that is yet to reveal itself. And I experience this not as a form of wishful thinking but more from the notion that because there are no random occurrences, nothing is happening without cause, its true purpose and benefit will surface in due time.

I could list countless examples of living by this principle even before I learned to meditate. What's different now is the confidence that every unfavorable circumstance is bound to change with the ripening of time and proper understanding.

The wisdom expressed in "Things always work out in the end and if they haven't, then it isn't the end" beautifully sums up another way to think about seemingly upsetting things that eventually turn out to be set-ups for something beneficial down the road! And sometimes "eventually" is a few hours or days, or a few weeks or months, and can also be a few years or decades away.

No Coincidences (Or Karmic Connections), p.7
Optimism in Impermanence, p.15
Everything Is Perfectly Timed…, p.19

Personal Reflections

Galloping Wants Outpace Needs

That there is often a gap between one's needs and wants, necessities and indulgences, is not a novel concept. The insight that has emerged for me, however, is how these can evolve insidiously over time without warning or ill intent.

Allow me to elaborate with a personal example.

Upon completing college, I arrived in the United States to pursue my graduate education and was fortunate enough to receive a full-freight scholarship to cover the cost of my tuition, living, and boarding expenses. Without this financial assistance, I couldn't afford to receive the much sought after higher education in the Western hemisphere.

I vividly recall how elated I was to find out that I would be entitled to a healthy monthly stipend, which truly felt like all the money in the world at that time and more than adequate means to cover my material needs as a doctoral student. In fact, I had no difficulty maintaining a very comfortable lifestyle well within that budget, which included shared housing, a used automobile, leisure activities, social meals, vacations, and even annual trips to India to see family.

During one of my meditation retreats, it occurred to me that the same amount that would tide me over adequately for a month's worth of living expenses is about the same I typically spend now in a single day when on a family vacation without much fanfare or compunction. Granted that my original baseline was over two decades ago and modest inflation alone would grow that amount by a quarter and my expenses at the time were solo and now are for a family of three. Yet, even with quadrupling my graduate student budget to account for inflation and a growing household to make it comparable to present circumstances, it still leaves a whopping ten-fold gap between my consumption at the time relative to present day!

What drives this gap and why does it seem so benign and uneventful a development and yet staggering at the same time?

My simple conclusion is that as we progress in life, we always have a certain set of basic *needs* that can allow us to subsist comfortably, and yet we always have a set of *wants* that we have our sights on longingly, and we keep striving to get within reach of such desires that offer the promise of fulfilling our dreams for a better existence.

Interestingly, as we make reasonable efforts over time, these wants not only come within reach but we start accomplishing them with increasingly greater ease and then start treating them as relatively essential needs. At the same time, because needs are needs and wants are wants, a new set of wants will surface once the prior ones are achieved, whether they be a better house, a fancier automobile, more children, nicer vacations, more time off, a higher salary, private schooling, country club memberships, and the list goes on.

What was till recently only a "wish list" item, starts to feel like a necessity. I remember reading a newspaper article that was genuinely empathizing with the plight of Manhattan millionaires that were having a particularly challenging time during the global financial crisis as their seemingly essential living expenses were drowning them into debt or forcing them to downgrade their lifestyle due to their bonuses being withheld even as their salary alone would otherwise be adequate to sustain five median income American households!

This insight has snapped me back to the realization that we examine the truly essential aspects of modern-day living. Non-rural housing, basic education, adequate nourishment, means for commuting, reasonable leisure travel, social meals, and the like can actually be managed fairly modestly without having to overreach into our available means.

What has also become clear is that unless we are vigilant, our wants will keep outpacing our needs and thus constant diligence is required to maintain perspective on what are true necessities and what can we live without, now or forever, if we embody a mindset of sufficiency and contentment.

The reason this is relevant is not only in the context of financial well-being as a mundane objective but also because this mindset enables us to live into the ideology of "renouncing" even within the context of modern living, without too much difficulty, and further aiding us on the path of inner development.

I recently came across a quote by Beop Jeong—a modern day renunciate monk often hailed as the Thoreau of Korea—that brilliantly sums up the essence of this gem in one simple sentence. "The key to happiness is not in how much we possess the things we need, but in how much we free ourselves from the things we do not need."

The Quadrants of Life, p.167

Personal Reflections

System Turbulence

Challenges occur even in the lives of serious and committed meditators. No one is completely immune to the vagaries of life and even the Buddha had to deal with them during his time despite his fully enlightened state of being.

The journey of meditation is a life-long (if not many lifetimes long) pursuit and thus must not be abandoned when turbulence arises in one's external environment or in the mind. Ironically, it is when we find ourselves in the midst of such a storm, that the practice can come in particularly handy and allow us to drop anchor in the middle of the ocean to find our footing. All too many of us lose the consistency of practice in these periods for a range of reasons: some because they find apparently less time to devote to it as it seems to take them away from dealing with the situation more directly through outward action, others because the heightened agitation they are experiencing due to the external strain makes their mind too restless to allow them to sit and remain on the cushion, while others may start doubting the efficacy of this noble practice as the mere manifestation of turbulence is evidence to them that meditation can't help overcome real life challenges after all.

My experience and learnings in this regard have been two-fold. First, we can't expect overnight miracles. We have now been meditating for a portion of our lives and to expect that it can offer us complete, certain, and permanent immunity from agitation or perturbation is unrealistic. One must keep ripening in the practice and make steady progress towards a more evolved and balanced state of mind over days, months, years, decades, and perhaps lifetimes.

Second, while our life circumstances may not change immediately, our ability to deal with them enhances through continuous practice of meditation. In fact, these turbulent events serve as grist for the mill to test and aid in the development of long-term equanimity. If we only experience smooth sailing or only minor bumps along the way, we miss out on building the ability to truly dampen the inner oscillations caused by (seemingly unfavorable) external stimuli.

If we manage to carefully observe our mental activity during such periods, we discover that veiled behind even such intense turbulence is the realization and experience of impermanence in all life phenomenon and thus arrive at the optimistic conclusion that "This too shall change." And through this understanding, while we may not be able to reduce the choppiness of oceanic waves on a windy day, we can at least learn to surf and keep our heads above water most of time and simultaneously enjoy the ride!

Optimism in Impermanence, p.15
Change Is Good, Change Is Inevitable, p.75
Change Is Hard, Change Is Easy, p.79

Personal Reflections

Ehipassiko – Come, See for Yourself!

It is said that there are two unmistakable signs when one is making real progress on the path—the first is an immense sense of gratitude for anyone who becomes an instrument in helping us find the Dhamma and the second is the noble volition to help others taste the same nectar of wisdom one has received, leading to immense benefit.

The noble volition to introduce any new acquaintance to the spiritual path becomes stronger as we derive greater merit from the practice of meditation. Assisting others in their journey onto the path benefits us through the principle of reciprocity of good deeds.

For people who may be unfamiliar with the benefits of Vipassana meditation or those who remain skeptical even when they learn about it, the Buddha simply invites them to come see for themselves instead of engaging in intellectual debate. *Ehipassiko,* in Pali, means "Come, see for yourself!"

Thus, when logical persuasion or other skillful means don't work, we simply invite those uninitiated to come and experience the benefits for themselves on their own and not because the Buddha said so or we may say so. The best and only real proof point of a technique working is when one experiences its benefits directly. Any other data point like reading or hearing about the value of the technique would be second hand anyway.

Often, out of concern for some who could draw benefit from learning the Dhamma but are unwilling to take the first step on the path for any reason, we may run the risk of going too far in trying to convince them to try out the technique. The best thing for us to do is either allow them to be naturally inspired by noticing the benefits in those whom they trust and respect, or better yet, simply give the technique a direct and fair trial on their own.

Ehipassiko rings true every time. In my personal experience in urging others to learn Vipassana meditation, all have said that going on a retreat was beneficial, whether or not they subsequently opted to pursue the path more fully.

The Buddha categorized people into three types as it pertains to walking on the path of Dhamma.

First are those who will at least receive the gift of Dhamma in their lifetime. Second are those who either had the seed from before or have gained it in this lifetime, and strive to ripen further on the path with the germinant seed. Third are those who will remain bereft of the Dhamma in this lifetime.

Aside from serving as an example of living a life of purity, peace, and equanimity ourselves, the foremost way for us to pay forward the gift of Dhamma we have received is to invite others to its doorstep and allow them to draw their own conclusions once they experience it for themselves. *Ehipassiko.*

And whether someone pursues the path beyond the first introductory course or not, for us to become an aide in them at least receiving the seed of Dhamma in this very lifetime is a highly meritorious deed.

When the Student Is Ready, then the Teacher Appears, p.3
Ripen on The Path, p.199

Personal Reflections

Untie the Knots and Free the Mind

Often people wonder where to enter the path and how to start the process of liberating oneself from the trappings of this unsatisfactory life form. The simple answer is that the moment you stop tying more complex knots in your mind, the pursuit of liberation automatically begins.

As I have started to journey on the path, I have found that my mind had been a fertile swamp teeming with such complex and deep-seated impurities that I wondered how long it would take for me to clear out these conditionings and progress towards a more serene and clean slate. Interestingly, at the outset, meditation simply serves to keep us from reacting to situations in unwholesome ways that create further mental complexes. These complexes make it harder to clean out the toxicity hardened deep inside since it has piled up in heaps upon heaps over long periods of time. Once we stop adding to the pile, slowly but surely the process of removing the layers becomes easier and occurs on its own as we keep making progress on the path.

Consider the analogy offered by the Buddha of a rope that we have been twisting from both ends and has now become quite tightly and complicatedly wound up into a seemingly intractable mesh. Rather than figuring out where and how to start the process of disentangling it, if we simply let go from either or both ends and stop tying ourselves up in further knots, the rope naturally reopens and straightens out spontaneously. All we had to do was to stop the process of generating more toxicity to start reversing the accumulated morass that was making us miserable.

What I have also found is that the journey on the path is not linear, as with everything else in life. There are times when I am only making incremental progress, while other times I progress in leaps and bounds, and yet other times I feel that I am actually regressing. And yet, having tasted the nectar of pure Dhamma and experiencing its potent benefits firsthand, all I have to do is to remind myself of those beneficial qualities to keep myself motivated to stay on the path even as obstacles arise.

Just as I don't question when I make unexpected improvements, I also no longer question when insurmountable hurdles come my way as I know deep down from firsthand experience that following the path is the only logical and tractable option for gaining inner peace and happiness.

Non-Linearity of Life, p.173

Personal Reflections

Open to Possibility…
…and Not Enslaved to Plans

Whether in mundane worldly matters or in the context of inner development, the need to make the requisite effort to pursue one's goals is self-evident. What comes naturally with that construct is the need to develop plans into the future. Without concrete plans with clearly outlined actions, milestones, and associated timelines, it would scarcely be possible to approach and achieve any goals—big or small.

This gem is simply offered to encourage the reader to allow for serendipity and spontaneity to provide (positive) intrigue and unexpected (often non-linear) gain.

Too often we are so enslaved to our original plans that when something unplanned appears, seemingly different and unconnected to our goal, we might ignore its presence, even when it is staring us in the face, and we do our best to evade or resist it, staying committed and beheld to our initial thinking.

We might still make it to our planned destination with continued effort and dedication alone, but we might miss out on an opportunity for serendipity to provide a more creative, streamlined, or simply more enjoyable solution to our goal. There are times when keeping our mind open to (and welcoming of) possibilities might seemingly take us away from our previously desired objective but there is potential bounty in that mindset.

The well-known quote from the famous General Dwight Eisenhower reminds us, "In preparing for battle I have always found that plans are useless, but planning is indispensable." I draw two relevant and correlated parallels from this military wisdom which also applies in our personal lives.

First, the discipline of planning is critical whether it is during times of "peace" (no particular major challenge) or during times of "war" (when pursuing a particular mission). Without the ability to plan out options and scenarios, we can easily be thrown off our game and we need the foresight to be able to handle surprises and unexpected developments.

And second, while it is important to form well-developed plans as a form of insurance, it is also wise not to hold onto them as dictums that one must follow as life doesn't turn out as planned and one must leave room for (if not expect and accept) new possibilities.

There is beauty and ease in holding our intentions gently and remaining open to the possibility that if better attuned to what the universe puts forward, we may progress further to an even loftier goal.

Do Nothing and Achieve Everything…, p.11
Seeing Is Believing, p.55
Non-Linearity of Life, p.173

Personal Reflections

Scaling the Mountain of Inner Purification

Upon achieving the sought-after highest level of positional success in my chosen profession some years ago, I found myself experiencing a mix of emotions from elation and relief to aimlessness and lack of motivation.

And after the celebrations and accolades had been received and acknowledged, the unsettling feeling of "Now what?" kept me agitated for quite a while and I was somewhat embarrassed to admit how the achievement of a lofty worldly goal was leaving me with feelings of emptiness and purposelessness on the inside.

My community of fellow journeymen on the path of meditation came to the rescue in the form of liberating counsel from one of the senior teachers. His advice in a nutshell was if I was struggling to find the next outward mountain to climb in the corporate world, it was time to single-mindedly and whole-heartedly commit to scaling the mountain of inner purification now that I had no other material achievements to strive for or prove to anyone (including myself).

The counsel came at a good time and served as the final missing piece in the mental jigsaw puzzle on how to complete my life's work having been fortunate enough to achieve everything I had set out to do in the professional context.

Whether one's pursuit of inner purification with a full embrace arises after satiating oneself from the trappings of worldly pursuits or comes into focus even as other material advancements still hold our interest, it remains the greatest service one can do for oneself and others while also bringing greater meaning to other aspects of life.

As I continue to work to further integrate and more deeply embrace the path of purification of my mind through a life of meditation and service, what I also find happening spontaneously is that my external circumstances are also improving and enabling me to pursue these dual objectives with greater ease.

It is also becoming clearer that removing defilements from one's mind to decondition it to its natural, happy, compassionate, and friendly state is far harder than any professional achievement. Daunting as that may seem, it has the one benefit of being a goal that doesn't easily turn stale. What is comforting and confidence-inspiring is the experienced knowledge that with even the smallest step forward, I am getting nearer to the ultimate and most pursuit-worthy goal of scaling the mountain within.

Inner Purification Leads to Outer Alignment, p.109
Follow Your Inner Compass, p.119

Personal Reflections

Dwelling in the *Metta*-Verse

While it is likely that humankind will continue to pursue alternative or altered forms of reality through virtual or imposed means as a form of escape from our mundane existence—and providers of such services will feed off of the dissatisfaction we experience in a real world—a different universe of positive energy is available to us if we can tune our inner antennas to the forces of *metta.*

Metta is a Pali word which means loving-kindness or generating and sending friendly vibes towards others. Most of us (meditators or otherwise), can naturally try to cultivate feelings of harmony and kinship towards others as we aim to live a peaceful life in a social construct. What is noteworthy, however, is that through purifying one's mind of defilements such as greed, fear, anger, hatred, or lust, our ability to attract this fount of friendly vibrations continues to rise and then such energy flows freely from our being through compassionate acts and sympathetic joy.

As our own sense of individualism, in an egotistical manner, diminishes through the realization of the universal nature of unsatisfactoriness that we all suffer from, our ability to harmonize and resonate with the feelings of others increases progressively to a point where we no longer draw boundaries between joy or sorrow experienced by oneself or another.

And the proactive process of channeling the energy of *metta* through oneself creates a multiplier effect of such positive forces being drawn towards us and us towards them. We then start to more easily shed any negative experiences as they appear incoherent relative to the feelings of abundance from inside the broader universe to which we find ourselves more connected within.

If you have a contemplative practice of any kind and haven't yet discovered the benevolence of *metta,* or even if you are not a meditator, experiment with bringing its essence into your daily life. If you are already a practitioner and yet feel you are not quite getting the hang of cultivating *metta,* I encourage you to stick with it and also keep deepening your foundational contemplative practice. Our ability to send and receive *metta* is directly linked to the purity and peace we experience within ourselves from cleansing our minds of the negative conditioning. Removing these negativities opens the entry to your own *Metta*-verse.

Personal Reflections

THIS LIFETIME

The Tripod of Life

Through years and years of near incessant effort towards progressing in my life journey on the basis of academic and professional achievement, I had come to the simple-minded conclusion that my ability and focused effort were the sole determinants enabling my life's outcomes. Applying a Newtonian approach to the life journey, I believed that the force and energy I applied would directly and proportionally propel me forward and thus believed the greater my effort, so shall the output be.

One of the biggest emergent insights through meditation has been that I was only viewing the picture partially. I now believe that there are three distinct and equally important legs of the tripod that dictate outcomes in all aspects of my life. In order, these are starting point, environment and effort. In other words, it is a proportional combination of where we enter a situation, what the contextual (supportive or unconstructive) forces surrounding us are in that set-up, and finally how we apply ourselves against the challenge at hand.

Back to academic achievement as one personal example to illustrate this concept. If I had not been born to parents who valued education as highly as mine did, nor had the volitional means to provide that learning opportunity, I would have been at a one-third deficit going into life (aside, naturally, from whatever innate abilities I came into the world with). Yet another third would have gone unaided had it not been for the caring support of teachers, mentors, friends, and relatives who helped nourish and cherish me throughout. So too the schoolmates with whom I had a special bond as kindred spirits, aunts and uncles who were great educators and took a deep personal interest in chiseling the raw intrinsic ability, or academicians in school and college who pushed me to be the very best that I could be while showering unconditional and unwavering support.

It is only the final one third that can be attributed to the effort I put into shaping my journey and it is even hard to say if I would have cultivated the effort or mindset had it not been for the first two ingredients: starting point and supportive environment. With this approach, it would be easy to take the glass half-empty (or more precisely two-thirds empty in this case) view of the situation as one can believe that since only a third of the outcome is derived from my effort, why try too hard? Quite the contrary, this insight has actually helped me take the glass is one-third-full approach in that if I only really control a third of my destiny through effort, I must triple my energies so as to maximize output on at least that score!

I find that these three ingredients actually support and build on each other in inexplicable ways. For instance, the more I strive and invest time towards an objective or aim, the "starting point" for any future efforts becomes inherently stronger. The more I strive with a strong volition, the universe draws me towards like-minded people (and them towards me) who share the same noble purpose, which increases the "environmental support" I receive for my efforts to be successful.

Establishing an understanding of life's tripod has been a big and revelatory personal unlock. On the one hand, it has put my mind at ease that I can't be too obsessed with outcomes and their correlation to my effort alone, since there are two other factors that contribute to my life's outcomes. On the other hand, however, it has fueled greater effort on my part since that is really the only leg of the tripod that is in my direct control.

Personal Reflections

Follow Your Inner Purpose

One of the most unexpected developments that has occurred through cultivating a meditation practice is that I have finally been able to tap into the well of inner wisdom and better identify and clarify to myself what my raison d'etre is in this lifetime. I have read countless self-help remedies and motivational books where the author expounds upon the notion of aligning one's efforts with one's sense of purpose as the single biggest breakthrough to bring life satisfaction and effortless success at one's chosen objective.

It always made sense intellectually that if you make your vocation something you inherently believe in and enjoy then your work will become fun and the proverbial "running to work every day" would be a natural consequence. It also felt intuitive that one should naturally focus on what one believes in, as anything else would be a form of intentional deprivation, especially when external circumstances are not a constraint.

Despite all these sensible reminders, I always had two struggles with this concept. First, just *how* do I know or go about truly and confidently identifying my inner purpose? And second, even if I *somehow* know what my inner calling may be, just how do I go about pursuing it within the constraints and expectations of my current life context?

I'll take these each in turn and link back to how a life of contemplation might help resolve the conundrum.

I suppose that most of us come through adolescence with a range of fleeting ideas of "what I want to be when I grow up". I recall wanting to be a pilot, a military officer, a school teacher, a professor of mathematics, and a professional cricketer!

Somewhere along the way between the reality-checks of my innate abilities, parental influence, peer pressure, the cut-throat competitive environment growing up in a country with limited opportunities, I ended up with a mainstream goal of achieving technical prowess as an engineer. Also along the way the notion of actually identifying and caring about my purpose fell by the wayside and I became one of the countless people striving simply to acquire a good education and seek a decent job (or further higher education) upon graduating from college. I still maintained some clarity about the types of things I didn't want to pursue though the spectrum of acceptable options remained relatively wide.

To summarize this part of the story, I got carried by the current and ended up becoming a management consultant. Despite a highly technical doctorate in science and engineering and consciously eschewing business education, I came to be reasonably good at my chosen trade (or I might say the trade that chose me!) Somewhere along that way, I started enjoying it sufficiently as there were aspects of the profession that really appealed to me like counseling clients, which was somewhat akin to my long-standing interest in teaching, even though it wasn't in a classroom context. I enjoy coaching them more on how to be a strong leader and less to impart them technical knowledge.

Upon my introduction to meditation, a few things quickly became very clear. First, I genuinely (more than accidentally) enjoyed my profession and it was something I wanted to continue pursuing, now more so as a conscious choice instead of allowing it to remain a default setting out of inertia. I appreciated the nobility of my vocation more as the essence of it was to enable others (whether individual, or the institutions they represent) to become more effective, stronger, and successful.

Second, I wanted to bring greater purpose to the choice of activities I would conduct within the broad realm of my responsibilities. This would manifest in the form of being more selective about the nature of clients I would serve—their mission, their institutional or individual congruence with my own value system—and the types of colleagues I would want to associate myself with and enjoy serving clients with.

Finally, the more novel insight was the realization that there was more I could uniquely do to help my colleagues (and professionals more broadly) to draw benefit from purifying their minds through meditation and living a more balanced, fulfilling, and sustainable life. I was also gifted with the emergent wisdom to not go headlong into this third aspect of my inner purpose as the idea of bringing this to the masses had to be filtered through the notion of taking a middle-way and avoid the extreme of evangelizing too much as it would be a turn-off for people on the one hand and also run counter to the idea of approaching such noble pursuits with a detached mindset, free of achievement orientation.

Subconsciously reflecting on my purpose during periods of meditation has led me to the clear and confident realization that I must continue to live in the real world of business as my primary vocation at the present time. What has arisen is the volition to discharge my duties in a manner that is aligned with the notion of serving others—whether through assisting them in aspects of their mundane existence or in the noble pursuit of a more evolved sense of self. In fact, the platform my current professional context affords me—to influence the senior-most echelons in the corporate world—is probably providing a unique set-up for me to make the biggest contribution by enhancing the personal and institutional effectiveness of these important leaders, towards whom society and their employees look up to as role models.

As such, I have gratefully and cheerfully concluded that I too have the option to pursue my inner purpose having finally discovered it, courtesy of meditation, and experientially understood what the masters have always known—that aligning one's purpose with one's actions brings effortless outcomes and joy. Identifying and serving our inner purpose is an opportunity that awaits us all and in many ways is both a privilege and an obligation.

The only (slight) caveat I would impose on this ideology is that it is not advisable to pursue one's purpose in a manner that is at odds with one's family needs or situational, societal context. I call it a *slight* caveat because as one ripens sufficiently in the practice of developing insight into oneself, it also comes with the wisdom of *how* to pursue this purpose in a balanced manner and in harmony with one's current life context.

The beauty, however, is that as one starts to pursue one's truest inner purpose in whatever manner—big or small, slowly or quickly, intensely or partially—the universe starts to rearrange one's life circumstances spontaneously such that a door opens up automatically for us to walk through with ease and alignment.

Inner Purification Leads to Outer Alignment, p.109
The Tripod of Life, p.157

Personal Reflections

The Quadrants of Life – Learning, Earning, Returning, Renouncing

Let me add a fourth phase to the frequently cited learning, earning, returning cycle amongst the entrepreneurial world and connect this analog to a concept popular in defining the optimal lifespan in the traditional context of living a life that comes full circle with the final stage of renouncing.

Regardless of how long one may expect to live, I find it helpful to think of life in these four, somewhat sequential, phases. A good chunk of our initial life into early adulthood is spent in imbibing knowledge, whether in a classroom setting or in the crucible of one's real-world experiences. It is then but natural to turn towards acquiring, whether more knowledge, wealth, prestige, power, or relationships during the earning stage of life.

It is easy and tempting to stay focused on this aspect and try to stretch this out to however long possible by craving greater amounts or quality of these outward achievements. And yet, especially once our own material needs are well met, devoting time in service of others as a form of returning can bring far greater joy than any added material pursuit. Turning inwards through meditation or introspective contemplation can enable us most easily to identify and connect with our inner purpose or calling becoming the foundation of our service orientation. Renouncing is naturally the most inscrutable and scary prospect and yet it follows naturally and gradually as one moves the balance of effort towards returning and as such retaining less and less for oneself.

While there is no set prescription to the duration of each quadrant, I find it easiest to think of it in approximately 25-year increments if one generously assumes a lifespan of 100 years, and also to keep the math simple!

As the essence and brilliance of the quadrants plumbs deeper into my mind, especially as I approach (if not likely already beyond) life's mid-point, I feel a greater pull to devoting the second half (however long or short that might be) to returning and renouncing. In fact, gradually dialing up these aspects even sooner in how I currently spend my time feels like an essential ingredient in leading a fulfilling life.

These phases also match up nicely with societal and familial roles we are required to play during our lifespan to be a contributory member in our communities. We have greatest capacity to learn and grow during our early years as a child and young adult. Having had the benefit of this acquired knowledge or capabilities, we can apply ourselves in service of society to yield output for others and earnings for one's household as we mature as adults and into our mid-life.

It is also easiest to start and raise a family during these years both given the natural biological, emotional, and financial capacity one possesses in this phase of life. And when one's responsibilities towards family start to diminish, while still having adequate physical strength, one can start the process of returning to society in the form of service and charity and also begin turning towards inner development. This then leads us smoothly to the stage where we can begin to renounce most worldly trappings and focus entirely towards a life of contemplation and in service of others seeking to journey on the path.

All in all, enabling a fulfilling and balanced life.

That life is non-linear is not lost on me so I accept the counter-argument of trying to view these as quadrants of a pie and not necessarily the quadrants of a timeline which can all be cultivated proportionally at any time during our lifespan. And yet, I see the wisdom in thinking of them as phases, with some overlap because they line up nicely with how the human body develops, flourishes, produces, and then deteriorates, decays and eventually dies.

Naturally, it's never too soon to inculcate aspects of inner purification and service to others even while being committed to learning and earning as dictated by life context. In my own case, I find that starting on this journey while squarely in my earning years, has enabled me to be firmer and more confident in my commitment to devote the second half to returning and renouncing. As I start progressing toward the returning aspects, I find that the idea of eventually renouncing is starting to feel more and more tractable. I feel increasingly comfortable that my needs will diminish and I will both be able to live off less and be less attached to what I possess or presently hold dear in a material context.

I am grateful to have been fortunate enough to acquire the means and be able to increasingly overcome the insecurity of whether I will have sufficient financial independence when I am ready to turn the tilt further in the inward direction. What I have concluded is that whatever amount we think is necessary to feel comfortable, or any goal that we set, it can never be enough nor account for every possible eventuality to give us complete peace of mind unless we don't inherently possess (or cultivate) a mindset of contentment and detachment. I have every confidence that the universe will provide for my every need without me worrying over it.

The Universe Provides (For My Every Need), p.43
Galloping Wants Outpace Needs, p.127

Personal Reflections

Non-Linearity of Life

Wouldn't things be so much easier and simpler if life progressed in a straight line and in a predictable manner? As everyone can attest, nothing could be further from that expectation. And yet despite these lived experiences, we continue hoping, praying, and wishing that things turn out the way we want them to, when we want them to, and manifest in a certain manner. How much fret and struggle when that turns out, often enough, to not be the case.

If one steps back from it all, it's easy to conclude even in a mundane manner that life's events and trajectory is inherently non-linear. Even when making progress, it is often two steps forward and one step back or sometimes more steps backwards (or sideways) and only a few in the "right" direction.

It can even seem at times that one's overall journey is heading in a downward or "wrong" direction and we find ourselves questioning the divine merit during such perilous or confounding periods in our life. We rarely ever doubt the universe's intent when the developments are reversed in their appeal, and we are unexpectedly or undeservingly propelled forward with little or no effort.

Here's how I have drawn meaning in (and from) the non-linearity of life.

We expect things to follow a linear logic when there are only a few pieces of input that predicate the expected output. Think 1+1=2. Even in something as predictable and dependable as arithmetic, we advance to the concept of non-linearity when multiple variables are involved and the relative importance of these variables is not equal. Try $1^1 x 2^2 x 3^3 = 108$! To the mathematically uninclined or uninitiated, the above equality (referred to as a hyper-factorial) might appear like black-magic as to how a handful of small numbers can possibly create such a large result.

Incidentally, the number 108 is significant in many Indian religions. For instance, in the Buddhist context, this number is the product of the six senses (sight, smell, sound, taste, touch, and mind) with the three types of experiences (pleasant, unpleasant, or neutral) with the two sources of their generation (internal or external) with the three time frames of occurrence (past, present, or future) bringing us to 108 different feelings (6x3x2x3 = 108).

In Hinduism, the number is considered auspicious for a variety of reasons and as such, there are 108 beads in the prayer rosaries. The oldest known ancient Hindu scriptures, the Upanishads, are 108 in number.

To amplify strength in unity, people often use the phrase "1+1=3", or the version I prefer, "1+1=11", inspired by the Hindi catch-phrase that spells out that equality to dramatize the value of the simpler version, that implies that sometimes when two things come together in a powerful and complementary way, the output is greater than can otherwise be expected intuitively, thereby hinting at the potential non-linearity or the inexplicable variable that creates the multiplier effect.

If we look at the nearly infinite factors that impact our every move and action in terms of starting point, environment, and effort, it will become easy to conclude that we can hardly expect anything in our lives to follow a straight line.

Even going to the grocery store can have surprises like unexpected weather changes that might slow us down or an important food item being out of supply that might force us to rethink the dinner menu, let alone things like completing one's education, which can offer lots of twists and turns along the way.

The knowledge that life is non-linear can actually be a liberating insight if viewed in a positive light. When we align ourselves with the wisdom and will of the universe, it need not be an unsettling realization that we can't predict what comes next.

My appreciation for this gem came with the realization that all life outcomes and long-term trajectories tend to be relatively evenly distributed in the favorable, unfavorable, and neutral orientation. When I feel stonewalled in a pursuit despite repeated and well-meaning effort, I step back and accept that the timing (or even the essentiality) of that outcome may not be right in the first place.

If I'm being truly honest, up to now I have received far more in life than I have distributed to others or returned to the universe. And thus, despite any non-linearity, life and the universe have been very kind to me even if it may not seem as such in a given moment. In fact, I feel a debt of gratitude for all of life's blessings and feel that I must continue to look for ways to pay it forward.

As I continue to reflect on this gem of apparent non-linearity, I do often wonder if but to the all-knowing universe that these life phenomena are rather intuitively governed by some higher order calculations than my limited mind can grasp.

As such, the apparent decelerations in the journey of life are increasingly as welcomed and meaningful as the accelerations, and the confidence that I am marching steadily towards the ultimate goal doesn't leave room to bemoan any unexpected hurdles along the way.

Do Nothing and Achieve Everything…, p.11
Dhamma Willing, p.47
The Tripod of Life, p.157

Personal Reflections

The Other Quadrants of Life

Another set of four personal priorities that are somewhat orthogonal to the quadrants of learning, earning, returning, and renouncing that have clearly emerged over the last decade plus are the touchstones of family, profession, exercise, and meditation.

I have found that when I am adequately nourishing all four aspects, life seems to progress smoothly and fruitfully. And when any one of them is out of balance, it tends to impact all the others and starts to strain the overall equilibrium. I state these four that apply to me and could be somewhat unique and specific to an individual.

At a macro level, I see three intersecting frames or lenses from within which these four are most prominent in my case. These are mind, body, and purpose or spirit.

Each of us have our own set of ingredients to the recipe of personal balance and well-being. I have concluded that there are in fact ten possible ingredients that classify under these three categories. These are sleep, exercise, nutrition, family or relationships, hobbies, meditation, professional calling, role in society, introspection, and spiritual connection.

I share this longer list only to highlight that the most prominent ones for each of us may well be different and perhaps it is essential that one's own signature recipe include at least one each from the categories of mind, body, and purpose, for it to be well-balanced and holistic.

Another aside on this list is the notion that one can only really thrive when some essential structural factors are in place. These include professional stability, financial security, comfortable housing, and child or elder care for those who have young or old dependents.

Back to my own list of quadrants, I am reminded time and again of the importance of servicing each of them well and simultaneously. These are not linear or sequential and failure in one area does cause a domino effect on all others.

Let me share a recent example of a sports injury to my back that caused me to step back from strenuous exercise, which I very much cherish. Despite nothing else being out of order in other life aspects—work going rather well, family life as good as ever, and continued benefits from Vipassana meditation—I found that the lack of physical activity at the level I am accustomed to started to impact my mood and life outlook.

Suddenly, I found myself confronted with proposed compromises from the medical community to switch to less impact sports like cycling and swimming relative to my mainstay of squash and distance running. This further heightened a sense of foreboding about future age-related bodily decline.

At a practical level, the lessened and varied physical activity led me to put on a few extra pounds, which probably started to cause mental lethargy. And the downward spiral of not exercising which then goes hand in hand with poorer nutritional choices started to kick in. I found myself being more irritable and less fun to be around for my family as

I would often be redirecting the conversation to my injury and how it was impacting my day-to-day life.

Loving family members, devoted as they may be to our well-being, certainly don't enjoy the company of a complainer and eventually tire from extending unconditional sympathy. This started to put a strain on what were otherwise very enjoyable relationships. I also found myself less excited by my otherwise very fulfilling line of work.

It wasn't until I found the right physical therapist, and I specify "right" as in someone who was right for me, that I started to reverse the spiral into a virtuous one. Slowly but surely, I set foot back onto the squash court, solo hitting at first and doing drills then lighter warm-up games with supportive friends, and then putting my running shoes back on for short, light jogs around the neighborhood. Finally I started to feel the clouds of morbidity lifting from every other aspect of my life.

That I was meditating throughout this health episode was an important and necessary touchstone that helped me keep things in perspective but an insufficient enabler in and of itself to restore my complete well-being.

It was an important reminder for me that these four quadrants represent the irreducible core of essential activities for me to feel complete as a person and thus fulfilled in all aspects of life at once. At the risk of sounding a bit "all or nothing", I would urge us all to self-discover what constitutes the bare essential scaffolding around which we can build the super structure of our thriving lives and guard them dearly at all times.

And when high winds threaten to blow it away, as they most definitely will from time to time, know that your formula to restore well-being involves bringing back vibrancy to each quadrant. I know in my case, the perfect equilibrium is rather delicate and hence continued diligence on sustaining the health of these quadrants offers rich and lifelong dividends.

Personal Reflections

Beget Merit, Avoid Regret

As a child when I struggled with making choices, I often wondered what principle to embrace in order to avoid regret after proceeding with a particular action. It was clear to me that success and happiness would be maximized if there was less second guessing and future regret but I didn't have a singular, clear and consistent governor to guide optimal decision making.

Getting introduced to the world of meditation reestablished the foundational importance of a moral code of conduct in a robust and absolute manner around five essential tenets. These are, in order:

1. Abstain from killing and harming others
2. Abstain from stealing or taking what's not given
3. Abstain from sexual misconduct—which implies infidelity or non-consensual relations
4. Abstain from false speech—which includes not telling lies, exaggerating or understating information, back-biting, and slander
5. Abstain from all forms of intoxicants.

These principles comprise the basic elements to ensure common people (not monks and nuns who are expected to adhere to yet higher standards) are able to live life in harmony with their environment and society at large.

The essence of these precepts is based on a simple principle that guides us to choose wholesome action versus unwholesome in all of our dealings. In as much as we can conduct ourselves by avoiding what's unethical or harmful, we protect ourselves from the downside associated with that choice.

Correspondingly, if we in turn choose a wholesome path in decision making, not only do we avoid any negative consequences but we in fact earn ourselves some karmic merits for doing the right thing and by serving the interest of others.

In other words, being able to honor two simple provocations—"Will this action of my mind, body, or speech harm myself or anyone else?" and "Might this action of my mind, body, or speech serve to benefit myself or others?"is all the protection we need to ensure we are choosing benefit over harm so that positive outcomes boomerang back to us in the future, thus begetting merit and avoiding regret.

Another practical reality that ought to urge us in this direction is the uncertainty and duration of one's life. Since death or disruption could uninvitingly knock on our door at any time, it is prudent to plunge ourselves into doing good deeds while we still can and accumulating merit from them.

~❀~

Kamma Vipaka - Actions Beget Outcomes, p.31

Personal Reflections

No Time Like the Present

Where and how one finds time to devote towards cultivating an inner life through the practice of meditation is often a threshold question that arises in the minds of new meditators—or those yet to be introduced to the practice—and creates an obstacle to starting on the path.

The simple answer is that *now* is the best time to devote to your meditation practice. People fall into the self-fulfilling trap of concluding that they don't have time to practice and thus wait for a more opportune time in their life to pick up meditation or even if acquainted with it, only delve into it with a small toe in the water.

What I have discovered is that committing to one's practice automatically and naturally starts to create the space for it in our lives. The sheer intention of doing so will offer you time that you didn't believe was otherwise available, never mind the benefits of the practice itself attuning your mind to be more drawn to it. There is no gimmick or superstition implied in this statement. Once you discover the cleansing, nourishing, and recharging benefit that meditation bestows on your mind and mental faculties, it is hard to turn away and regress in your commitment. Humans are wise enough to pursue interests that bring them lasting value in their lives and meditation ranks high on that yardstick once it has been properly afforded an opportunity to demonstrate its efficacy.

In my case, a few of the practical things that have spontaneously and seamlessly occurred that are aiding me in this regard are that my sleep requirement has perceptibly reduced and I also find myself a lot less drawn to mindless escapes like watching hours of television. The first one has helped me unexpectedly become an early morning person, allowing easily for an extra hour before the usual start of my day to devote to my practice. And the second one has afforded me more time in the evenings to have a second meditative recharge at the end of a long day.

To be sure, I am not advocating sleep deprivation and also acknowledge that everyone's requirement differs. I have found that my meditation practice also provides my mind a certain amount of mental rest while being awake even if my body is not lying down. Sufficient sleep is a necessity and no one knows it better than me—as a chronic asthmatic, I know too well that lack of sleep can promptly trigger a health episode—and yet despite that I have found an equilibrium that allows sufficient time to meditate and also derive adequate nightly rest.

What is necessary to overcome the initial (and to an extent ongoing) inertia is that one must taste the nectar in full measure through a proper introduction to the chosen type of meditation. Too many people, looking for quick fixes and instant miracles even when convinced about the potency of the technique, will only take an approach of, "I'll meditate when I can find the time," or start out with a few minutes at a time.

Anyone who takes their health and fitness seriously doesn't just exercise or follow a healthy diet "when they can find the time" or for a few minutes at a time. Much in the same way, for meditation to manifest its power to relax, detoxify, and unleash the mind, we must pursue it with requisite time, effort, and consistency. People who take their workout routine seriously will orient their entire day and week around ensuring they devote adequate and regular time to it instead of fitting it into what's left available after other activities consume the majority of their schedule.

The popular analogy of needing to first fit in the highest priority "rocks" into a finite container of your valuable time before allowing the "sand" of incrementally important chores—instead of going about it the other way around—applies to choosing meditation as a central priority if you are to live life by the principle of focusing your time on what matters most.

Personal Reflections

Ekayano Maggo – The Only Way

This esoteric sounding Pali phrase simply conveys that there is only one way to purify our minds to rid us of the defilements that keep us from living eternally peaceful and harmonious lives. This particular reference is made by the Buddha to the Noble Eightfold Path where he outlines the unassailable set of essential ingredients to methodically pursue and achieve salvation through one's own efforts.

It may seem a bit overconfident, if not a little arrogant, to proclaim that this is the only way to free sentient beings from the continual cycle of unsatisfactoriness and misery. Perhaps his unshakable belief came from lived experience and having tried all sorts of other methods (including certain austere penances) to rid his mind of cravings and aversions before rediscovering Vipassana meditation, which in its essence is a step-by-step approach to remove all the mental conditioning that binds us.

From personal experience, while I am yet at the very early stages of walking on the path legislated by the Buddha, the nature and extent of positive changes—both mundane and supra-mundane—that continue to appear through my meditation practice provide ongoing proof and encouragement that every little step I take leads to immediate and lasting benefit.

The proof being in the pudding, as the idiom goes, the Buddha invites us all to come see for ourselves (*ehipassiko*) and believe only what we can corroborate with our very own lived experience, as that's the only reality our mind can truly and fully accept. It may seem like a huge leap of faith to believe that the path he laid out is the only efficacious path available. As such, I recommend that whatever contemplative practice we find appealing and suitable to us, that we pursue it to a level of proficiency that we can assess its effectiveness for us.

A few commonsense yardsticks to assess whether a chosen spiritual path is efficacious and beneficial.

1. The most elemental aspect of any path that is worth following is a strong foundation in a moral code of conduct. A baseline of ethical behavior is a necessary precondition for quieting the mind, which in itself is essential to spiritual progress. Any technique that advertises freedom from basic moral principles like truthfulness, non-harm to others, and avoidance of sexual misconduct, must be treated with suspicion and caution.

   While certain methods proclaim efficacy without adherence to essential morality, these are merely bound in delivering their practitioners pleasant experiences without actually eradicating the source and generation of dissatisfaction in one's life.
2. The technique needs to be universally applicable and not limited in its application or appeal to a certain sect of people. If the technique can only serve a selection of human beings—whether based on their religious or philosophical beliefs or level of intellect or any other distinguishing feature—then it fails to have the quality to remedy true suffering. Since suffering is universal, so must be its remedy!

3. Another test of its purity is that practicing the technique should not bring any harm to others. After all, what good would our inner development be if it comes at the price of adversity to those around us?
4. Importantly, the results from practicing the technique ought to be immediate in the here and now (*akaliko*) and not limited to some time frame in the future—be it the time of death or, for those who can believe in the possibility, in future lives.

   If the only proof of the utility of a technique to truly purify our mind lies far out in the future, how can we be certain about its efficacy in the first place, and why will people practice it with diligence when they can't see results in a reasonable time frame or altogether in their lifetime?
5. One must also examine the motivation, self-adherence, and virtue of those imparting the teaching of the technique. Are they truly steeped in living their life in accordance with the principles of what they teach and themselves practice? Do their own mannerisms reflect the benefits they proclaim come from the followership on the path they legislate? Are they maintaining the sanctity of the teaching by not turning it into a form of livelihood, or worse, treat it as a commercial transaction? These and many such questions that assess the purity of their volition must be answered satisfactorily before surrendering oneself to their discipleship.
6. Another watch out for those truly seeking a proper path and associated doctrine is to be careful not to fall prey to gimmicks and those offering instantaneous, often miraculous, results.

While a suitable path must deliver benefits here and now, anyone promising effort-free gain is either under an illusion themselves or certainly trying to create one in the mind of another. Progress on the right path must always be accompanied by the proportional amount of effort and certainly must be pursued by oneself and cannot be gifted to us, even from a super-being.

While a self-realized (or fully-enlightened) person can show us the path and outline in detail what its followership entails and how to assess one's progress in a stepwise manner, even they can't hand us liberation on a platter.

If any technique (and those practicing it) meet these conditions, then we can be relatively certain that it can be of true liberating benefit to us and put wholehearted effort in pursuing it without any doubt or concern. Naturally, our ongoing commitment to a chosen path can only come from observing carefully the changes that manifest directly into our lives as a result of its practice. Any rational being will only pursue something with reasonably strict adherence when they experience the value it delivers to them firsthand.

Speaking from personal experience, I have found the practice of Vipassana meditation to meet the tests of foundation in ethics, universality of appeal, freely available access, non-harm to others, immediacy of benefits, and the purity of its teachers. These are in addition to the ongoing and sustained benefits I have directly experienced as a result of its practice, deepening my confidence in pursuing it.

For those not already committed to another path that is serving them well, I recommend giving Vipassana a fair trial. Through my own lived experience, I certainly now believe it is truly the only path, having tried a handful of others and wandered aimlessly for years before stumbling upon this liberating technique. And rather than experimenting endlessly with a plethora of possibilities, and lose precious time during this human lifespan, I have fully and permanently committed myself to walking on this path through to its natural and final goal.

Seeing Is Believing, p.55
(Don't Lose) the Privilege of Being Human, p.203

Personal Reflections

Ripen on the Path…
…and Awaken the Germinant Self

It is said that each and every one of us sentient beings carry within us the seed of future enlightenment. And whether we develop a little or a lot towards that lofty and distant-seeming goal, there is value in making whatever progress we can in this very moment and in this very life.

Most of us, as I was, are either genuinely unaware of this prospect or even when aware, too inhibited by inertia or ignorance in making even the slightest effort in the right direction. Some might miss the opportunity altogether because they never encounter this liberating path throughout their lifetime.

For those fortunate enough to have the soft knock of opportunity on their doorstep that often occurs through serendipity, I would urge each and every one to seek the path and take the first step, however daunting or uninteresting as it may seem.

While clearly the journey on this path cannot occur without the necessary timing and karmic readiness, it is quite possible to gently part the clouds that are blocking even the faintest ray of warm sunlight reaching our frigid minds.

Once the spark has been lit, it is our privilege, opportunity, and obligation to ripen on the path and awaken our potential self. I emphasize obligation because it is only human beings that have the ability to introspect through meditation and walk on the virtuous path of inner purification and development, and, as we can see around us in the planet, the human form is not the most common relative to all the species that inhabit it.

While some of us will only fulfill the important yet limited step of receiving the seed of enlightenment in this lifetime, those who have inherited it from their past have the opportunity to establish themselves fully and firmly in a life of meditation.

And what gives us the impetus, confidence, and sustained energy to do so?

For one, whether we believe in future lifetimes beyond this one where we may flourish yet further due to the good deeds of this lifetime, the important learning and benefit we receive is that as soon as we start purifying our minds, benefits start appearing immediately and abundantly in this very life, thereby demonstrating the efficacy of the technique and engendering our resultant commitment to it.

What's more, the moment we commit to the practice ever so slightly, all sorts of visible and invisible forces come to our aid and clear the thicket of undergrowth further and pave the way forward in a supportive and self-reinforcing manner.

And as we take baby step upon baby step, despite getting knocked down or tripped up from time to time, should we choose to get up and resume the journey, our confidence grows as does our ability to be resilient, which further facilitates the clearing of the glide path.

The more confident we become, the baby steps turn into ambling strides, to leaps and jumps that spring us forward towards the ultimate goal, all the while heaping us with direct and spontaneous benefits in the form of equanimity, joy, compassion, friendliness, and generosity.

So, while it may be hard to know how much further each of us must travel or for how much longer to reach our destination, every step and furlong is filled with virtue and beatitude.

When the Student Is Ready, Then the Teacher Appears, p.3

Personal Reflections

(Don't Lose) the Privilege of Being Human

Caught up in the constant endeavor of striving for more or simply surviving the burden of life that many often feel, be it due to self-inflicted problems or truly unavoidable challenges, many of us fail to cherish the most fundamental advantage we have inherited as a species, and that is the privilege of being human.

It takes a little stepping out of our man-made microcosm to notice the inherent benefits we have been bestowed upon us as a gene pool of organisms. Aside from surrendering to the intense forces of nature, humans have clearly established their dominance over any other species on the planet. That fact alone confirms that we possess a higher level of intelligence and problem-solving ability that we continually harness to counter any form of hardship.

Whether it's having a more evolved language ability to the greater size and anatomy of our brain or the ability to move on two feet or the facility of relatively peaceful coexistence as a populace or having a moral code that is reasonably well-adopted, humans are advanced in most, if not all, aspects of life relative to other visible living entities.

There is, however, one unique aspect of being human that many lack knowledge of or under-appreciate even if aware of it. It is our ability to introspect. No other species possesses a highly evolved ability to look at itself with this kind of self-reflection or in a self-evaluative manner.

This is a particularly special feature as it offers us the possibility to meditate in a way that allows us to methodically remove (and even fully eradicate) defilements that make us miserable on a day-to-day basis and also stand between us and the possibility of lasting peace and serenity. And whether one believes that each of us appeared on this planet as a human rather than a dog or a butterfly, it behooves us to contemplate that what our mental wiring affords us is something to put towards good use and not fritter away.

Life is short and fleeting and the possibility of being human is a rare occurrence. Losing the chance uniquely available to us to gain insight into ourselves to free ourselves of negative conditioning would be a real pity. We must constantly remember to cherish our existence as an inheritance that we have the obligation and the opportunity to use well to multiply and advance the meritorious deeds that enabled us this privilege in the first instance.

Cultivating an inner practice is certainly one way we ensure we are discharging this responsibility in an opportunity-filled manner to live up to our full potential as a species. The benefits of doing so will be self-evident and self-reinforcing enough—we just need the initial activation and then a supportive environment to strengthen this blessing into a continuing and lasting endowment.

Personal Reflections

Self-Author Your Last Chapter (Now)

So many of us are continually figuring out what the next chapter in our life ought to be. The race towards the perpetual "what comes next" starts fairly early in life. From one school year to the next, to sports and extracurriculars, to college, to the first vocation, to career transitions, to romantic interests, to starting a family for those so inclined, to raising and educating children, to the first owned home, to wealth accumulation, to retirement planning, to care-giving for elders, and on and on and on goes the treadmill of life. It's almost as though we are yearning for something beyond the present moment or treating the phase of life we are currently in as just a temporary stopping point.

Another notable aspect of this endless pursuit of "next is best" is the amount of effort we put into setting ourselves up for success in that future endeavor. We study, we seek counsel from mentors and teachers, we consult others who are already in that phase, and some even pray to higher powers for divine intervention to maximize our odds of receiving a favorable outcome.

It only occurred to me recently that other than bemoaning the prospect of, and planning financially and medically for it, what little true advance preparation we do towards the final chapter of life, which is the moment we pass away from the body we inhabit for an entire lifetime!

Oddly, in some way it may behoove us to be even more proactive and planful for this moment because despite all the advances in medical science and technology (including predictive algorithms and artificial intelligence), no one can pinpoint with any precision when someone's time is rendered complete from this particular bodily mold of their consciousness.

What's more, we delude ourselves in expecting the best outcome at this stage of life contrary to every other one where we put ourselves to the grindstone of effort and continuous striving to ensure favorability. Why? Because it is dreadful to think about it in the first place and is probably genetically coded in us to not obsess over dying because the constant agony over its prospect would paralyze us on a day-to-day basis.

Ironically, however, pursuing a spiritual path at whatever stage in life is the equivalent of buying a life insurance policy that is guaranteed to pay off in that *known* moment of future need. Any spiritual path that is endorsed without any reservation by its past practitioners is built upon the foundations of reducing one's ego and sense of unhealthy attachments to any object, person, or ideology during one's lifetime. This importantly includes the inherent attachment to our physical and mental self—the body and the mind—and the notion of a separate entity or individual personality that we so dearly hold onto during our lifetime.

While we intellectually accept that we can't take any material belongings with us when the moment of passing arrives, the actual preparation for it—which is truly ridding oneself of the need for any belongings—is left unaddressed by most, until often the very end. Even the littlest effort we put into this development, whatever one's chosen path, will pay huge dividends in the future.

And though I can't comment on it from lived experience, I can say that my fearfulness towards death has started to diminish, something that I (like most) had inherently dreaded in the past. I credit this new outlook to my chosen inner path.

Personal Reflections

Adding the Secret Ingredient

If the insights, ideas, and stories in the preceding pages have intrigued or inspired you, I would offer one final gem for your consideration which is the fount of all this experiential knowledge. And that is the gem of Dhamma and the benefits that come from living life in congruence with its principles. The endeavor of purifying one's mind through learning and practicing Vipassana meditation with regularity and commitment is the primary vehicle for this pursuit.

Each of us has the seed of awakening within and the opportunity lies ahead for us to protect, cherish, and nurture it. The benefits of doing so can be profound with immediate results showing up in our mundane life, let alone the incalculable karmic merits we will enjoy and retain as we move forward towards the ultimate goal of complete liberation.

Following the path chartered by Dhamma allows us to live with greater purpose, harmony, equanimity, compassion, and joy. Every day brings forward new opportunities for us to grow and glow in virtue on this noble journey without forsaking any mundane responsibilities or expectations.

Vipassana meditation has been around for millennia and in some ways might appear to have been a well-kept secret given the limited number of people who were practicing it in its pristine form since it was widely unavailable over the centuries in most of the world. Fortunately today this secret is a readily available universal remedy for one and all regardless of ethnic background, religious belief, or social standing. And so, I urge you to add this secret ingredient to the recipe of your life and unlock the door to inner joy.

~ ❁ ~

Ripen on the Path…, p.199

Personal Reflections

Acknowledgments

Akhilesh Bhandari
Anand Dhelia
Bob Kegan
Brihas Sarathy
Daniel Vasella
Deepak Chopra
Dominic Barton
Florence Wilson
Jane Gladitsch
Jim Medrano
Kalvin Kochhar
Kory Goldberg
Michael Fisher
Nalin Ariyarathne
Nishant Chaudhary
Nitin Chawla
Pooja Vasudev
Scott Keller
Steve Hanlon
Vineeta Chopra

About the Author

Manish Chopra is a senior partner at the global management consulting firm, McKinsey & Company, where he counsels CEOs and advises boards on their most strategic issues. He has served prominent mission-based healthcare institutions across North America, Europe, Asia, and the Middle East over his 23-year career with the firm. He also served as the managing partner for McKinsey's Singapore office from 2010 to 2012.

Manish experienced a personal transformation in 2010 through learning Vipassana meditation. This led to the publication of his first book, *The Equanimous Mind*, which chronicles his initial experiences with meditation and the positive impact it has had on his personal and professional life. The more recent tenth-year anniversary edition of the book is enriched with updates from his ongoing journey of sustaining impactful changes.

Aside from his role as a professional and a family man, Manish devotes a meaningful amount of time in championing the message of inner personal development and cultivating one's well-being within his firm and through public speaking at business, government, and academic institutions. He also continues to serve the organization responsible for enabling new and preexisting Vipassana meditators to learn and build upon their practice of meditation.

Manish grew up in India and attended college at the Indian Institute of Technology in Delhi before completing his Masters and PhD from the University of Michigan in Ann Arbor. He currently lives in New York with his wife and daughter.

Out of gratitude for the benefits received from the practice of Vipassana meditation, Manish donates the proceeds from his books to spreading awareness about the technique, so that others can draw value from it as well.

ABOUT PARIYATTI

Pariyatti is dedicated to providing affordable access to authentic teachings of the Buddha about the Dhamma theory (*pariyatti*) and practice (*paṭipatti*) of Vipassana meditation. A 501(c)(3) non-profit charitable organization since 2002, Pariyatti is sustained by contributions from individuals who appreciate and want to share the incalculable value of the Dhamma teachings. We invite you to visit www.pariyatti.org to learn about our programs, services, and ways to support publishing and other undertakings.

Pariyatti Publishing Imprints

Vipassana Research Publications (focus on Vipassana as taught by S.N. Goenka in the tradition of Sayagyi U Ba Khin)

BPS Pariyatti Editions (selected titles from the Buddhist Publication Society, copublished by Pariyatti)

MPA Pariyatti Editions (selected titles from the Myanmar Pitaka Association, copublished by Pariyatti)

Pariyatti Digital Editions (audio and video titles, including discourses)

Pariyatti Press (classic titles returned to print and inspirational writing by contemporary authors)

Pariyatti enriches the world by

- disseminating the words of the Buddha,
- providing sustenance for the seeker's journey,
- illuminating the meditator's path.